BABBITT

including
- *Life and Background*
- *List of Characters*
- *Summaries & Critical Commentaries*
- *Character Analysis*
- *"Technique and Content in* Babbitt*"*
- *Suggested Essay Topics*
- *Selected Bibliography*

by
Gary Carey, M.A.
University of Colorado

INCORPORATED

LINCOLN, NEBRASKA 68501

Editor	Consulting Editor
Gary Carey, M.A.	*James L. Roberts, Ph.D.*
University of Colorado	*Department of English*
	University of Nebraska

Cliffs Notes, Inc.   Lincoln, Nebraska

CONTENTS

BABBITT
Notes

LIFE AND BACKGROUND

As one reads *Babbitt,* one is continually aware of Sinclair Lewis' fierce anger with America's mediocrity, a mediocrity usually expressed by a multitude of cliches. Lewis thinks that too many Americans often say the things that they are expected to say, that they act exactly as they are expected to act, and that they are extremely conventional as far as individuality and originality are concerned. It is as though the Americans whom he describes were living in a very expensive, pleasantly colored, standardly designed, cliched 1920s Dark Age.

Ironically, the facts of Lewis' early life are also cliched; they follow a trite pattern, one that Lewis himself would probably have agreed is seemingly almost required for a creative talent.

Born in the small, provincial town of Sauk Centre, Minnesota, in 1855, Harry Sinclair Lewis grew up in a sternly disciplined home. A strong sense of responsibility and seriousness were early instilled by Lewis' doctor-father. When Lewis' two older brothers grew up, they followed their father's choice of profession and became respectable doctors. But Lewis did not fit this pattern; instead, Lewis followed another pattern. From the first, he was a precocious child, a creative child. He was an unhandsome young boy—red-headed, unathletic, shy, and self-conscious; he was lonely and spent much of his time reading. When he was about eleven, however, he began writing and never stopped.

During the summers of his last years of high school, Lewis worked alternately on two newspapers and began to publish poetry. At Yale, Lewis continued to write, but other than some of the English faculty who encouraged him in his literary pursuits, he had few friends. After his freshman year, Lewis temporarily abandoned his studies and went to England on a cattle boat. It was an unhappy experience, but on his return to Yale, Lewis again buried himself in writing and produced a substantial number of essays, poems, and short stories. Then there followed another trip to Europe, a stay at Upton Sinclair's socialistic community in New Jersey, a try at supporting himself as a free-lance writer, and a trip to Panama. Finally returning to Yale in June, 1908, he finished two semesters' work in a little over one semester and received his degree.

Once again Lewis attempted to support himself by writing and, this time, he was able to do so, but his career as a recognized writer still seemed no closer. Lewis published an adventure novel for boys, *Hike and the Aeroplane;* his short stories fared well; and, in 1914, *Our Mr. Wrenn* appeared. It was a mildly satiric novel about "the little man" in America, the man who battles his anonymity and triumphs.

After *Our Mr. Wrenn,* Lewis published four more novels, all investigating Lewis' concept of what it means to be "American." In these early books, Lewis wondered aloud about the fate of the American spirit that pioneered and built a nation but now had no more frontiers to conquer. Lewis underlined the question by experimenting with such techniques as exaggeration, broad understatement, and irony. Still, however, in spite of his investigation of America, Lewis seemed to remain largely unknown.

In 1920, Lewis was no longer unknown. When *Main Street* was published, the press and the public were loud in both praising and damning Lewis and his novel. Overnight, Lewis became a controversial figure throughout America. Before *Main Street,* no American novel had attacked the much-romanticized myth of the small town. Lewis, however, was reared in a small town and felt strongly about the fraud of a small town's hominess and honesty. He meant his novel to dissect the narrow mediocrity of small town frauds – and he succeeded.

Two years later, in *Babbitt,* Lewis again staggered America – this time, with his portrait of the bourgeois businessman who achieved success and money and rewarded himself and his family with the most modern, material things his nation offered, but remained dissatisfied and confused.

Today, of course, *Babbitt* is an American classic, and the word "Babbitt" is a part of the American vocabulary; the word carries the unsavory connotation of someone who conforms rigidly to the standards of one's social peers, someone who is respectably middle class and has little social conscience and even less imagination.

After satirically depicting a typical small town and a typical suburban businessman, Lewis next turned his attention to medicine in *Arrowsmith* (1925); to religious quackery in *Elmer Gantry* (1927); and to Americanism vs. Europeanism in *Dodsworth* (1929). In 1930, Lewis was rewarded for his exhaustive study of America by being awarded a literary prize never before given to an American: the Nobel Prize for Literature for the entirety of his work. Ironically, the prize came at the peak of Lewis' career; from 1930 on, Lewis never again wrote a novel that had the impact of his early masterpieces. *Ann Vickers* (1933), *Cass Timberlane* (1945), and *Kingsblood Royal* (1947) were financially successful and were all adapted for either the stage or the movies, but critics found the novels inferior to the masterful quintet of novels produced before Lewis was awarded the Nobel Prize.

Lewis also sensed that his writing no longer had the strength that he tried for. His subjects continued to be controversial, but his professional stature was waning. He was beginning to be obscured by other American talents – Thomas Wolfe, Thornton Wilder, Faulkner, and Hemingway. Lewis began drinking heavily, and after being unsuccessful in his marriages, he died alone in Rome in 1951. His last novel, *World So Wide*, was published posthumously later that year.

LIST OF CHARACTERS (in alphabetical order)

May Arnold

A middle-aged widow; Riesling's lady friend in Chicago.

George F. Babbitt

A middle-aged real-estate broker. To some extent, Babbitt is merely a stereotype and a caricature of a middle-class businessman; this is particularly true in regard to his speech patterns, his political and social ideas, and the organizations to which he belongs. He vaguely senses that his life is not a good one, and blindly he strikes out, trying to assert himself and find happiness. Unfortunately, he doesn't have the courage or the ability to succeed and, despite his yearnings, he is destined to remain what he was at the beginning of the novel: a small-minded, intolerant, poorly educated conformist "leader of society," concerned primarily with appearances and prone to attack whatever he does not understand.

Myra Babbitt

A dowdy, middle-aged woman; she is a devoted and efficient housewife, but she lacks the imagination and feelings to understand Babbitt during his long period of discontent. She is much too impressed by her husband's aggressive personality and "brilliance," and she is too conscious of the conventions of the middle-class social world.

Theodore Roosevelt "Ted" Babbitt

The Babbitts' son, a teenager. He is a good mechanic and athlete, a poor student, and is concerned primarily with girls, cars, parties, clothing fads, and making money. He is just entering adulthood and already reflects some of his father's same dullness and lack of creativity. Ted is in the midst of his adolescent rebellion against parental authority, and, like all young men, he thinks that he knows more than his father.

Verona "Rone" Babbitt

The Babbitts' oldest daughter, recently graduated from Bryn Mawr. She feels smugly superior to most people in Zenith because of her education and sophisticated ways. She considers herself to be a sensitive, serious, and enlightened member of a new, radical generation, but most of her ideas are quite shallow and superficial. In fact, Verona is much like her mother, although she would never admit this fact.

Katherine "Tinka" Babbitt

The family's youngest child; she is a cute and intelligent little girl, but is rapidly becoming spoiled by her family.

Fulton Bemis

One of Tanis Judique's friends; a member of "the Bunch."

Sir Gerald Doak

A British industrialist whom Babbitt meets in Chicago.

Seneca Doane

An attorney and liberal candidate for mayor; a leader of leftist sentiment in Zenith. Babbitt comes under his influence for awhile.

Reverend Dr. John Jennison Drew

Minister of Chatham Road Presbyterian Church, which Babbitt attends.

William W. Eathorne

President of the First State Bank of Zenith; one of the town's richest and most influential citizens; he and Babbitt are members of the Sunday School Committee.

Kenneth Escott

A young reporter on the *Advocate-Times* who eventually marries Verona Babbitt. He is an undereducated, pseudo-intellectual college graduate, the masculine counterpart of the type represented by Verona.

Sidney Finkelstein

Babbitt's friend and a fellow club member; a department store executive.

T. Cholmondeley "Chum" Frink

Babbitt's friend and fellow club member; an advertising writer and nationally syndicated newspaper poet. (Note: "Cholmondeley" is pronounced "Chumley.")

Stanley Graff

Babbitt's outside salesman; he is fired after it is discovered that he has been cheating a customer.

Vergil Gunch

Babbitt's friend and fellow club member, a leader of the Good Citizens' League; president of the Boosters; Zenith's largest coal dealer.

Beecher Ingraham

A liberal minister; formerly a member of the Congregational Church, he is now devoted to the advancement of the working class.

Orville Jones

Babbitt's friend and fellow club member; owner of Zenith's largest commercial laundry.

Tanis Judique

An emancipated and bohemian middle-aged widow with whom Babbitt has an affair. He rapidly discovers that the conventions of her way of life are as stifling as those he is attempting to escape.

Eunice Littlefield

Ted Babbitt's girlfriend and later his wife; she is a caricature of a typical, teenage girl of the 1920s.

Howard Littlefield

Eunice's father; Babbitt's friend and fellow club member, as well as his neighbor. He is an executive of the Zenith Street Traction Company and holds a Ph.D. in economics; hence, he is considered an authority on nearly any subject.

Theresa McGoun

Babbitt's stenographer.

Charles McKelvey

A millionaire building contractor, one of Zenith's most influential people and a leader of the Good Citizens' League. He and Lucille, his wife, are the town's social leaders. The Babbitts attempt to climb the social ladder by inviting the McKelveys to dinner.

P. J. Maxwell

Paul Riesling's defense attorney.

Opal Emerson Mudge

Zenith leader of the American New Thought League.

Caleb Nixon

A leading businessman and colonel of the Zenith National Guard unit.

Carrie Nork

One of Tanis Judique's friends, a member of "the Bunch."

Jake Offutt

A corrupt and influential political boss.

Ed Overbrook

An unsuccessful college classmate of Babbitt's; he attempts to improve his social position through a dinner invitation to George and Myra.

Joe Paradise

Babbitt's Indian guide in the Maine woods.

Lucas Prout

A wealthy Zenith manufacturer. Babbitt assists in his successful mayoralty campaign.

Professor Joseph K. Pumphrey

Babbitt's friend and fellow club member, owner of the local business college.

Ida Putiak

A young manicurist with whom Babbitt has a date.

Paul Riesling

Paul has been Babbitt's closest friend ever since he and Babbitt attended college together. Paul is sensitive, introspective, quiet, and passive. He is unhappy because he was unable to become a violinist and because he doesn't have the strength of character to either control his wife or leave her. Paul's greatest weakness is that he lacks the moral courage to do the things he wants to do.

Zilla Riesling

Paul's wife. She does not understand her husband at all; she is selfishly concerned with her own needs and pleasures. She blames all her marital problems on Paul and is unwilling to share the burden of building a happy marriage. She is a merciless shrew and enjoys pretending to be a martyr.

Cecil Rountree

A wealthy Zenith realtor; leader of the delegation to the convention in Monarch.

Sheldon Smeeth

Choir leader at Chatham Road Presbyterian Church.

Colonel Rutherford Snow

Powerful owner of the *Advocate-Times* and a leader of the Good Citizens' League.

SUMMARIES & CRITICAL COMMENTARIES

CHAPTERS 1–4

Summary

On a morning in April, 1920, George F. Babbitt, a forty-six-year-old real estate dealer, awakens in his house in the exclusive Floral Heights section of Zenith, a medium-sized, midwestern city. Zenith is a typically expanding modern city with new factories and office buildings, modern homes, fine roads and express railroad service, as well as the usual slums and other urban paraphernalia.

Babbitt is pink-skinned and baby-faced, with a slight tendency toward heaviness. He seems prosperous, although he is a businesslike and unromantic person in appearance. He has awakened unhappily this morning – partly because he is suffering from a hangover following last night's poker game, and partly because, as usual, he has dreamed about a fairy girl with whom he is able to escape his dull, mechanical existence. This morning, he is forced to face reality and it takes him awhile to adjust.

Babbitt arises at 7:20 A.M. and carries out his regular morning ritual of washing and dressing. His actions and thoughts are the same as those on nearly every morning of his life. Myra Babbitt, his wife, also rises and begins her household duties. She is a chubby, mature woman, dressed in a housecoat. After a typical quandry concerning whether Babbitt should wear his brown or grey suit, he finishes dressing.

Before Babbitt leaves the bedroom, he views himself in the mirror and takes pride in his eminently respectable and executive-like bearing. He glances out the window and catches a glimpse of downtown Zenith, three miles away. The functional beauty of the tall, shining skyscrapers inspires him; he feels a nearly religious feeling of awe for the modern, urban way of life in America.

Babbitt's house is moderately expensive and modern. It has all the latest conveniences and appliances and was designed, decorated, and furnished by the finest and most stylish contractors. It is quite similar, both inside and outside, to nearly all the other houses in Floral Heights. The only fault with the Babbitt house, the author comments, is that it is *not* a home.

At breakfast, the Babbitts are joined by their three children – Verona, twenty-two, a recent graduate of Bryn Mawr and very conscious of her culture and sophistication; Ted – Theodore Roosevelt – Babbitt, seventeen, a student at the local high school; and Tinka – Katherine – ten, a somewhat spoiled yet sweet little girl. Throughout the meal, the family bickers about a number of minor issues. Babbitt is suffering from his usual morning irritability, and it is finally necessary for him to shout them into silence.

The children leave for school or work, and Babbitt sets out for the office. As he drives to work, he meets his neighbor Howard Littlefield, an executive of the Zenith Street Traction Company and the holder of a doctorate in economics. Howard is one of the most highly educated men in Floral Heights, and Babbitt is one of the many admirers of his learning. The two men engage in a short, cliche-filled discussion about the weather and current politics.

Continuing his journey, Babbitt derives an adventurous feeling of personal heroism from driving recklessly. At the gasoline station where he stops, the mechanic is attentive and respectful. This behavior, as usual, tends to increase Babbitt's self-esteem, and he becomes a bit more cheerful. As on all other mornings, the drive to work through the city's many varied and industrious districts excites and inspires him.

Babbitt's office is in the Reeves Building, a modern, downtown skyscraper. The Babbitt-Thompson Realty Company (Thompson is Babbitt's father-in-law) has nine salesmen and several office clerks, most of whom are already busily at work. For some unknown reason, however, Babbitt feels out of sorts this morning and does not derive the usual satisfaction from viewing the modern fixtures of his office. Nonetheless, he settles down to the day's business. He continues, however, to feel restless. Babbitt muses for a while about the fairy girl of his dreams, and then feels ashamed, for he is a highly respectable family man and has never yet done anything to endanger his reputation in the community.

As the morning progresses, Babbitt composes several additional advertisements, including a rather tasteless one for a cemetery of which he is the agent. These ads are written in tortured and misleading purple prose, but Babbitt is proud of them and considers them to be stylistic masterpieces. When this work is finished, he becomes bored and, as is his habit, he decides once again to stop smoking. Afterward, he telephones Paul Riesling, his closest friend, and arranges a luncheon appointment.

The remainder of Babbitt's morning is filled up with petty and routine details. After describing these, Lewis comments that Babbitt is a successful real-estate broker because he is reasonably honest and dependable, has a good sales personality, and is diligent. Unfortunately, however, like many men in his field, Babbitt is ignorant of the most elementary and important matters pertinent to real-estate, such as the principles of scientific sanitation, the nature of adequate educational facilities, police and fire services, and so forth. Nonetheless, Babbitt understands real-estate values, and he is not above making a slightly shady deal once in awhile if it is profitable and has an air of respectability. As a result, Babbitt's firm is one of the most prosperous in Zenith.

Babbitt is seemingly a highly virtuous man. He advocates and praises the wisdom of many laws, although he does not always observe them. He is a regular contributor to his church and other reliable charities. He does not believe in cheating—except when everyone else is doing it, or when it is necessary in order to protect himself.

The balance of the chapter contains a detailed account of the way in which Babbitt and Conrad Lyte, a local speculator, pull off a slightly dishonest real-estate deal and make a nice profit, at the expense of a helpless grocer in one of Zenith's residential districts.

Commentary

Lewis begins *Babbitt* by describing the setting—the city of Zenith—then placing the main character, George F. Babbitt, in the setting. The portrait is of an unimaginative midwestern America and its middle-class protagonist, and so Lewis introduces them in the best possible way: within the Babbitt-Zenith mentality. Already the standard of utility is at work.

Zenith, the city's name, is indicative of Lewis' attitude toward contemporary America. A zenith denotes a pinnacle, an ultimate, but if this city which Lewis describes is man's best effort, then the result is sorry and disappointing. Besides Zenith's towers—suggesting modern man's self-imposed prisons—man has built himself other meaningless and grotesque buildings. Mansard roofs "torture" the structures beneath. Everywhere in Lewis' description of Zenith, the houses and machines seem more alive than the people who use them.

It is dawn in the opening scene, but there are no bird songs; they have been replaced by factory whistles. The morning sun is "splintered" by the glare of steel. Man has created a monster, a metal forest hundreds of thousands of times his size. The enormity of man's creations have diminished man instead of doing what his creations were originally designed to do: ennoble him.

After a long-distance view of Zenith, Lewis focuses on the sleeping figure of George F. Babbitt. Asleep, Babbitt is not the solid citizen that he is when he is awake; instead, he is the remnant of the credulous dreamer that he was as a youth. And it is with this initial stroke of characterization that Lewis humanizes Babbitt. Granted that our first impression of the man is not wholly sympathetic, we never wholly forget that Babbitt – however fraudulent and hypocritical he proves himself to be – can dissolve at unguarded moments into a romantic who longs for peace and beauty (the world of the fairy child).

Babbitt's dream is threatened by the noises of milkmen, furnace men, paper carriers, and automobiles, and when the dream finally breaks, we witness the metamorphosis of the once-sleeping Babbitt into the now-awake Solid Citizen Babbitt.

Immediately on awakening, Babbitt begins to change. He takes strength from the fact that he is awakened by an expensive alarm clock. Significantly, the clock is one in which cathedral chimes have been shrunk to man's secular needs. In other words, cathedral chimes no longer call one to prayer; instead, they call one to work. And it is the price of the clock, not its tone, which pleases Babbitt most. Babbitt's god, Lewis tells us, is modern appliances.

Having mentioned modern counterparts of paradise and God, Lewis next turns his satire to the matter of sin in Babbitt's Theology of Things. Before breakfast, Babbitt battles the steel, chrome, and glass controls of the bathroom; he rails at his daughter's using a smelly "heathen" toothpaste; he slides against the tub and, frustrated, wipes his hands and face on a never-before-used guest towel. With this act, Babbitt commits a household "sin" and is censured by his wife.

Babbitt's metamorphosis continues. First, he was observed in bed in baby-blue pajamas; his wife awakened him by calling him "Georgie boy," and later, dressed in his BVDs, he still looks like a little boy. Slowly the facade is applied; note the words that Lewis uses to describe Babbitt's dressing process: adornment, embellishment, donning – words suggesting special, sacred vestments instead of the ordinary business suit which Babbitt is putting on.

After his suit is on, Babbitt pockets such trinkets as an elk's tooth, a pen, some keys, a knife, some notes written to himself, and again Lewis points out the seriousness of the task. These are Babbitt's modern-day holy medals. And besides the "holy medals," Babbitt carries the modern-day equivalent of a missal to guide his thoughts and deeds; he carries editorial clippings. His values are determined on the basis of printed dogma, learned by rote from his collection of newspaper editorials.

This particular morning, Babbitt continues to be out of sorts. He worries about his digestion, wondering why his apple-a-day has failed to keep him feeling fit. He worries until he looks out at the towers of Zenith. These towers of steel quiet his nerves; like silver, silent priests, they give him peace.

The Babbitts' house is described in much the same way that the Babbitts' clothes were described: both house and clothes are good, solid, and uniform; best of all, they are respectable. The house has an abundance of electrical outlets for lamps, for vacuum cleaners, toasters, and electrical fans, but between the Babbitts themselves, there is no "spark" of love. The analogy between the excess of modern electrical appliances, their outlets, and the Babbitts' lack of love seems obvious.

Myra Babbitt is described as being "as sexless as an anemic nun"; she bulges in corsets, fastens her clothes with safety pins, and takes no interest in her femininity. She treats her husband much as a fussy mother might. As for Babbitt, Lewis says that he appears "extremely married"; that is, the magic has gone out of his sex life with Myra. Babbitt is the man who pays Myra's bills; he is her solid citizen protector, but he is not her lover.

At the Babbitt breakfast table, Verona, a Bryn Mawr graduate, expresses her discontent with her paltry job as a filing clerk. Babbitt, however, is unconcerned about his daughter's desire to do something "worthwhile"; he is repulsed by Verona's naive dream of opening a small chintz-decorated welfare corner in a department store. "Rone," the Babbitt's eldest child, is a dreamer, and now that Babbitt is fully awake, he scoffs at dreams.

Ted, the Babbitts' second child, is also a dreamer. He dreams of shortcuts to success and also of becoming an adventurous secret agent. Neither of Babbitt's older children respect work as much as their father hoped they would. Ted's dreams and Verona's socialistic ideals are out of place in Babbitt's solid, common-sense household.

Commenting on the state of the world, Babbitt growls that "we got no business interfering with foreign governments"; then, seconds later, disgusted by a hint of change in the Russian power structure, Babbitt wonders why "we don't just step in there and kick those Bolshevik cusses out." Babbitt has no consistent system of values; however, *he* believes that his values are consistent for one reason: because he has worked hard. Hard work automatically equals wisdom in Babbitt's scheme of things. He uncritically quotes platitudes and scrap ends of editorials. Babbitt's mind only *seems* to think, just as the Babbitts' furniture only seems to be made of mahogany and the toilet articles only seem to be made of solid silver.

After Babbitt leaves for work, several things boost his spirits. On his way into Zenith, Babbitt has his car filled with gasoline, and, similarly, he stuffs himself with platitudes for the day. At the filling station, Babbitt collects the chatty respect of the attendant; all of these things – well-being, wisdom, and respect – help fill out Babbitt's image of himself.

Finally, one last quality – manly courage – is infused into Babbitt before he assumes his daily role of businessman. Besides the battle which Babbitt waged in his bathroom this morning, he wages two more battles before he checks into his office. He battles a streetcar (a valiant effort) and battles to park his car (a virile adventure).

Once Babbitt arrives at his office, the tones of Lewis' satire changes. It is no longer funny to watch Babbitt because now Babbitt is engulfed in a building filled with other Babbitts. All individualism has been removed, and it is from these offices that the energy that moves America is discharged. Here is the nerve center of Zenith's – and Babbitt's – money-making.

The motto for Babbitt's real-estate business is "Homes for Folks," an especially fraudulent motto because the houses which Babbitt sells are not "homes," nor do "folks" buy them. Lewis implies that they are cells for robots; the development, for example, at Glen Oriole contains neither a glen nor an oriole. Glen Oriole is merely a clever tag to snare prospective home buyers who dream of living in a glen with trees filled with orioles. But Babbitt's business functions – it sells houses and it makes money.

After sharply and satirically creating for us a picture of Babbitt's narrow-minded drive to make money, Lewis cajoles us into giving more sympathy to Babbitt. Babbitt is not a happy man. He is a frustrated man. Despite the fact that Babbitt's intellect and values have greatly atrophied, his sense of sex still flickers and underneath Babbitt's cliches and posturings, he is mildly alert to every pretty ankle he sees. We enjoy seeing that Babbitt is not yet an empty husk, that while he is able to calculate the cost of repapering a room, he can also calculate the cost of an inter-office affair with his chirpy-voiced secretary.

In Chapter 4, Lewis gives us a multitude of details about Babbitt's business ethics; then he ends the chapter with a long scene in which we see these ethics illustrated. We learn, first of all, that in Babbitt's code, a businessman is not acceptable if he is not sufficiently broad-shouldered, deep-voiced, and hearty-humored. Success is attracted to such manliness, and Babbitt's buying-and-selling business is, Lewis says, a "manly" business. Zenith is manly beauty to Babbitt; it is manly poetry literally measured by the height of its buildings. Babbitt responds to the poetry of the material – the shine of steel and the energy of restless automobiles.

Babbitt begins his day manfully; he is assertive, exercising his authority. His "Do You Respect Your Loved Ones?" is rhetorical, attempting to fill readers with guilt if they have not bought a plot in Linden Lane. Note, however, that Babbitt is not wholly untainted from things "un-manly"; he enjoys a fancy word or two and indulges in such purple-prose expressions as "daisy-dotted" and "smiling fields," even though most of his advertisement is written in "manly" prose.

Babbitt has made money; that is a fact. He is a success, so he is not completely ignorant of sales maneuvers. His right hand may scribble pretentious lures for real estate, but his left hand is realistically set on making money.

A quality of Babbitt's, pointed out already but particularly evident in this chapter, is his self-deception. A resolution to take better care of his health comforts him. Likewise, an unanswered letter that he intends to answer seems already answered; and instead of using will power and determination to stop smoking, he hides his cigars from himself. Babbitt, the great booster of will power, is a fraud.

Concerning Babbitt's business ethics, it is not surprising to learn that Babbitt's concern is not really for the community, as he claims, but for himself and the money he will extract. He "chants" lies; he has "ironed" a meadow into a sunburnt housing development, and he has bribed health inspectors and fire inspectors. And his excuse? He is "as honest as the next guy" – that is, he is "conventionally honest." In other words, he cheats only if cheating has been "sanctified by precedent."

Point by point, Lewis indicts Babbitt as a philistine, stopping only briefly for a point of humor concerning Babbitt's worrying about sewage disposal. Babbitt regularly boasts of the efficient sewage pipes beneath the Glen Oriole housing development, just as he regularly worries about his own bowels. Lewis notes that Glen Oriole's sewage pipes are not washed clean; they do not even function well; in short, they are very much like Babbitt's life. Both are full of stagnation.

In the scene involving the small grocer, Mr. Purdy, Babbitt's "conventionally honest" ethics are in full display. Babbitt's buying of land and offering it to the grocer at many times its value, disguising his greed as a gesture of friendliness, is fiendish. When Lewis has him call Purdy "Brother" and force cigars on him, Babbitt becomes almost too villainous. In this episode, Lewis' Babbitt is too hypocritical, too overbearing, and too greedy to be anything more than cartoonish — even after he collects his $450 commission.

CHAPTER 5

Summary

Before leaving the office for lunch, Babbitt hustles about importantly, giving unnecessary instructions to his employees. He lights a cigar, forgetting that he has just determined to give up smoking, and despite his many resolutions to get more exercise, he decides to drive to lunch, rather than walk three blocks.

As Babbitt rides through the busy downtown area, he observes the buildings and streets with fond familiarity. The city is really no different from many others throughout America, but to him it is unique and a source of pride. While driving, he reviews the morning's transactions with pleasure and evaluates his financial condition. He feels that his income is more than sufficient, but also that his family is guilty of much foolish and wasteful spending. Despite his decision to cut out needless expenses, he stops and purchases a costly electric cigar lighter for the car, feeling that even if he does stop smoking, this would be an impressive luxury to show his friends and clients.

Babbitt's luncheon appointment is at the Zenith Athletic Club, to which he and Paul both belong. It is the second most exclusive club in the city and all the most respectable business and professional men are members. Eventually Paul arrives, and when he and Babbitt enter the dining room, they are greeted boisterously by all their friends and are teased unmercifully when they decide to sit alone.

Despite his resolution to diet, Babbitt orders a heavy, fattening lunch. While eating, he and Paul discuss business and politics until

Paul finally confesses that Zilla, his wife, is still nagging him and that, as a result, he is beginning to despise her. He cites a few recent examples of his wife's cruelty and states that he is not satisfied with his life anyway, particularly because he always wanted to be a violinist and not a manufacturer. He longs to leave Zilla, but lacks the courage to do so. Babbitt and Paul have been friends since college and have a strong friendship. Although they are the same age, Babbitt has always viewed Paul as a younger brother and constantly seeks to provide him with a strong shoulder to lean upon. Now he gives Paul a good deal of conventional, moralistic advice that is of little real value, but nonetheless Paul gains confidence and faith from this display of friendship. Babbitt also tells Paul about the strange yearnings and feelings of discontent that he has been having lately. At Paul's suggestion, the two men decide that they will precede their families to Maine on their summer vacations in order to share some time together.

Commentary

Babbitt's club, the Zenith Athletic Club, is filled with fellow non-athletic Babbitts who use the club merely as a place to eat and talk. Clearly, the Zenith Athletic Club, like its members, is not what it appears to be. The members are not really friends; they are mechanized things. They are talking accessories of their mechanized houses, mechanically conversing with one another. Babbitt obviously needs them, but only in the way that he needs other mechanized things.

Concerning real people, Babbitt does have a need for one person in particular: Paul Riesling. Paul is an old friend and, in Babbitt's opinion, Paul could have been a great violinist or painter, but failed. Had he been successful in either of those fields, however, Babbitt would probably have had nothing to do with him. But, as it is, the two men are friends because they are contrasts — Babbitt, a successful businessman but a failure as a mature, independent-thinking man; and Paul, a moderately successful businessman but a failure as an artist. Paul is slim and is characterized by his hesitant speech; Babbitt is pudgy, pink, and characterized by his positive, hollow declamations. Thus Paul is, besides an old friend, a man whom Babbitt can feel infinitely superior to, can afford charity to, can excuse to his friends on grounds of everlasting friendship, and can confide in without feeling silly, weak, or inferior.

Babbitt confides to Paul about a matter which he can discuss with no other man: something is wrong. Babbitt is a success, has gained every material goal – nice house, nice car – and his family is exemplary (at least on the surface), yet Babbitt is unsatisfied. Paul, however, cannot help Babbitt. Paul calls Babbitt a "simp" (simpleton; a fool), then rails non-stop about his *own* life being unbearable. Ironically, it is Babbitt who must finally nurse Paul back into good nature. The confession scene is reversed. It is Babbitt who is left to heal himself, and he does so by lecturing Paul on "a man's duty" (magic words, to Babbitt, meaning "work hard and don't worry").

Far from being helped by his friend Paul, Babbitt is left frightened, yet thrilled. Paul's reckless mood is dangerous; Babbitt has dared Paul to kick out – to try and grab some real joy for himself. Vicariously, Babbitt also experiences a taste of recklessness. But Babbitt wonders: has Paul exaggerated the situation between himself and Zilla? Babbitt does not want his loyalty to Paul tested by an irresponsible act. Their talk dissolves with Babbitt uttering cliches.

CHAPTERS 6–7

Summary

After lunch, Babbitt returns to work and takes a prospective customer out to see a property. Afterward, he and Henry T. Thompson, his father-in-law and partner, go shopping for a new car for the older man. Babbitt is able to get a discount on the price through a fellow member of the Boosters' Club who is sales manager of the Zeeco Auto Agency.

Back in the office, Babbitt continues his daily routine. Late in the afternoon, he has an argument with Stanley Graff, his outside salesman. Graff has worked earnestly for Babbitt for a long time and regularly puts in extra hours. Now that he is planning to get married, he asks for an increase in his commission and a bonus for a particularly difficult sale that he has just completed. Babbitt angrily turns on Graff and gives him a stern, moralistic tonguelashing, criticizing Graff's lack of fairness, ideals, enterprise, and vision. Graff is not satisfied with this answer, but there is little he can do since Babbitt openly hints that he can easily get another salesman. Graff withdraws sullenly.

Babbitt feels guilty when he sees that the other members of his staff are sympathetic to Graff, but he will not alter his decision.

Babbitt returns home for dinner. As usual, the family squabbles about a number of small things, including the need for a newer and more stylish car. Babbitt promises to get one next year, but this solution only partially satisfies Verona and Ted. After the meal, Verona leaves to meet some friends; the others settle on the porch. Ted does his homework, Myra sews, and Babbitt becomes deeply engrossed in his favorite light reading, the comic strips in the evening newspaper.

After awhile, Ted begins to complain about the uselessness of the things which he is forced to learn in school – plane geometry and the works of Shakespeare, Milton, and Cicero. He says that he doesn't want to go to college because learning has no cash value; he is interested in making lots of money. He consults some ads for correspondence courses, ranging from fingerprinting to public speaking; all of them guarantee to increase one's earning capacity. His parents are impressed by the ads, but nonetheless they say that Ted must stick to his school work and go to college. A college degree has great material value in terms of social status and personal polish, even if the courses are dull and impractical. Ted willingly accepts his father's advice and then goes out to meet some friends, leaving his homework undone. Babbitt feels a warm glow of pride when he considers how adult and reasonable his son is.

After Ted leaves, Babbitt and his wife chat aimlessly for awhile about Ted's rapid maturation and his girlfriend from next door, Eunice Littlefield. Babbitt once again promises to have a heart-to-heart talk with his son someday about morality and manhood. For the rest of the evening, he reminisces about how he once aspired to be a lawyer and politician, but gave up these dreams in order to get married. He never claimed to love Myra, but they got along well, so, rather than let her be hurt, Babbitt married her. Myra has always been a good and faithful wife to him, although she is a bit unimaginative and unromantic. He feels sorry for her momentarily when he realizes that she too might have complaints or feelings of discontent, and he caresses her hair gently. Myra is surprised at Babbitt's gesture; it makes her happy.

As the evening continues, Babbitt and his wife sit in the parlor reading magazines. The parlor is furnished like most other parlors in the area, as well as those in most middle-class houses throughout

America. Soon, bedtime arrives and the couple goes up to their room.

While Babbitt is falling asleep, Lewis describes a number of things which are going on at that very moment in different sections of the city of Zenith. For instance, the wife of the town's richest citizen is committing adultery, a narcotics pusher in a fit of temper murders a prostitute, two scientists are up late in their laboratory conducting experiments on synthetic rubber, four leftist union officials are planning a coal miners' strike, an aged Civil War veteran who has never even ridden in an automobile lies dying, a tractor factory is working a night shift to fill a rush order, and a prominent, fundamentalist evangelist is just ending a tent meeting on the edge of town.

In another part of Zenith, Seneca Doane, a "radical" lawyer, and Kurt Yavitch, a histologist, are drinking and discussing the philosophical condition of contemporary America. At the same time, Jake Offutt, a political boss, and Henry T. Thompson are planning a crooked real-estate deal based on their secret knowledge of the projected extension of service by the Zenith Street Traction Company. They expect to realize a large profit from their illicit manipulations and plan to use Babbitt as their henchman.

Elsewhere in the city of Zenith, nearly 350,000 people are fast asleep. Most of them are unaware of the many things going on around them and many do not even care. In a slum near the railroad yards, a young man who has been out of work for six months kills himself and his wife. George F. Babbitt rolls over in his bed and dreams of his fairy nymphet, who offers him her hand and invites him to join her in an exotic midnight garden. She welcomes him eagerly, and, once again, Babbitt is gallant, wise, and uncritically adored.

Commentary

Lewis has shown us scenes of Babbitt in bed, Babbitt at breakfast, and Babbitt at business. Now he shows us Babbitt back home.

The Babbitts' evening meal is, as breakfast was, accompanied by quarreling. Again the subject is the same: the family automobile. Ted wants a new car because he wants to show it off; furthermore, Ted doesn't want to wait until he is his father's age to do so. He wants big money now, and he wants to spend it and show off. He wants a job that requires no study and no preparation, its only qualification being the desire for wealth, success, and adventure. Ted is looking for short cuts.

Ted is indeed his father's son – only more verbal and more naive. Babbitt is also a man of short cuts; he has exchanged original thinking and reasoning for the opinions of Howard Littlefield and the editorials in the daily newspaper. Ted does not want to earn financial success; Babbitt does not want to earn an independent mind. To Ted, Milton and Shakespeare and Wordsworth are "old-fashioned junk"; to Babbitt, poetry (and all art for that matter) are suspect – subjects that wasted a lot of Babbitt's time during his stint at State U. Ted finds beauty in chrome and horsepower; Babbitt, in Zenith's skyscrapers. There seems to be no real difference in their dreams, only in the focus.

At this point, Lewis allows himself some extra space for satirizing advertising copy. The springboard is Ted's praise of the Shortcut Educational Pub. Co. – a business that operates out of Sandpit, Iowa, an obviously unsuccessful address but a fact not considered by either father or son. The home-study courses promise many benefits – such as masterful originality, a quality that Ted will probably never have. And as for the "talking right up to the boss" idea, we have just witnessed Ted's father savagely upbraiding an employee who sincerely believed that he had a right to "talk up" and ask his boss for a better salary. Lewis' mimicking of the shortcut, get-rich-quick pamphlets is a tour de force, but it is pathetic that Babbitt cannot even begin to evaluate the leaflets that Ted is drooling over. Babbitt is such a run-of-the-mill, conventional fraud that he is unable to discern that these showy pamphlets offer nothing, that they too are fraudulent.

Babbitt's advice – that Ted get a college degree for prestige's sake in order to be able to associate with the best people, the best clubs, etc., – is one of the most damning things that Lewis puts into Babbitt's mouth. But Babbitt is only saying, in bold print, what many American parents think. They send their children to the best schools and colleges they can afford – not for the education, but for the prestige. They say they want "the best" for their children, but too often they delude themselves as to the meaning of the phrase, and for whose benefit "the best" is.

Only when Babbitt knots up inside, restlessly confessing that he wishes he'd been a pioneer, and then admitting that he couldn't be happy without his modern house – only then (and rarely does Babbitt have these insights into himself) are we responsive to the man. Most of the time, Babbitt is too monstrously mediocre for us to care about. But when Babbitt verbalizes his feelings of being lost, there seems hope for him — a chance for revelation as he peers into his inner self. But this happens infrequently, and we despair when Babbitt compares himself with his "lean Yankee" father-in-law and with the Princeton-educated Noel Ryland — and then declares that he, Babbitt, is a better man than either of them; he is the all-American mediocre man.

It would help us to care more deeply about Babbitt's fate in these first few chapters if Babbitt were more aware of what he has become. There is only passing reference, for instance, to Babbitt's early dream of becoming a lawyer, then governor of the state. Babbitt was a country boy with dreams, but he compromised for a job in a good-paying real-estate business and for a marriage to a "dependable companion." Babbitt, at this point in the novel, appears to be the embodiment of the American success story. But Babbitt's iron garage and his longing for the fairy child stain the immaculate surface of his vision of himself. Both irritants remain, and this section closes with Babbitt reverting to the child he was when he awakened. He plays in the tub with his shaving gear, making his cheeks youthfully sleek. He even shaves a swatch down his calf, creating a path of hairless, youthful skin. He readies himself for the fairy child — purifying himself, playing with the soap, lulling away the businessman persona, and then, out of the tub, he hastily says "Goodnight" to his wife and drops off to the land of the fairy child.

CHAPTERS 8–9

Summary

Two significant events take place during the spring of 1920. First, Babbitt is able to secretly purchase several real-estate options for himself and the company executives before the Street Traction Company publicly announces its plans to extend a particular streetcar line. The deal is sure to bring in a big profit. The other event is a formal dinner which Mr. and Mrs. Babbitt decide to give. They plan a real "highbrow" affair with evening clothes required, and for a long time all their energies are devoted to making plans for the party.

After several weeks of soul-searching discussion, the Babbitts conclude their plans for the dinner and select the final list of guests. They invite Chum Frink (the newspaper poet) and his wife, Mr. and Mrs. Orville Jones, Mr. and Mrs. Howard Littlefield, Mr. and Mrs. Vergil Gunch, and Mrs and Mrs. Eddie Swanson. All of these people are highly respectable and prosperous members of Zenith's upper-middle class.

The morning of the dinner party is one of confusion and chaos in the Babbitt household. An extra girl has been hired to assist the regular maid; Mrs. Babbitt is busy supervising and organizing the two servants; the children try without complete success to keep out of the way; and Babbitt is assigned the "responsible and manly" tasks of picking up the ice cream and buying the liquor.

Since this story takes place during the era of Prohibition, Babbitt has to drive to the worst section of town in order to purchase the liquor illegally. He is cheated badly by the bootlegger and treated condescendingly, but he accepts these embarrassments in a good-humored manner, for he takes secret pleasure in frequenting the haunts of criminals and having the courage to break the law.

Meanwhile, Mrs. Babbitt supervises the household chores. Babbitt returns from the office early and dresses in his evening clothes, although even that morning he said that he would *not* wear a "monkey-suit." The guests arrive, and after the usual latecomers finally turn up, the drinks are served. Babbitt has mixed the cocktails himself and, as usual, is proud of the masculinity which he feels this skill demonstrates. The guests have their drinks amid much jesting and gaiety, most of which is caused by the knowledge that federal law forbids the use of liquor. The men knowingly discuss Prohibition and rationalize that it is good because it prevents the shiftless working class from obtaining alcohol and thus becoming subject to all the vices caused by drunkenness. However, the men feel that respectable and reliable people like themselves should be allowed to drink whatever and whenever they choose, and that Prohibition is an infringement on their own personal liberties.

The meal consists of the foods customarily found at most middle-class formal dinners, and after dinner, everyone gathers in the parlor. Conversation of a very uninspired and conventional type ensues. The jokes which the men tell are crude and unsophisticated. Everyone seems to be having a wonderful and stimulating evening.

Chum Frink reads the group some of his latest poems and advertising copy. The poetry of advertising, he says, is far superior to any of the difficult, "longhair" stuff they were supposed to read in school – the "arty stuff" that foreigners and people who put on airs profess to appreciate.

Babbitt has always enjoyed being a host, and he has always been sincerely respectful of Frink's brilliance, but tonight something is bothering Babbitt. Meanwhile, the guests eventually run out of conversational material and start to grow restless until someone suggests that they play bridge. While a game is going on, Babbitt does something unheard of; he privately admits to himself that he is bored. This realization troubles him. He knows that he is hosting Zenith's most respectable citizens.

The interest of the guests in the card game is slackening when Mrs. Frink proposes that they conduct an experiment in spiritualism. They all gather around the table in the darkened dining room under the leadership of Chum Frink in order to hold a seance. Somehow Frink is able to make the table move. Everyone grows a bit uneasy, but they all try to seem unimpressed.

After the seance has ended, the guests chat for a while about spiritualism and psychic research, as well as the high state of American morality and the comparative quality of various makes of automobiles. Babbitt agrees with all that is said, but he is still bored and he quietly hopes that they will leave soon. Eventually the guests depart, after complimenting Mrs. Babbitt and enthusiastically assuring her that they had a wonderful time.

When everyone is gone, Myra proudly beams with pleasure and starts chattering about what a success the party was and how well everything went. Babbitt only half-heartedly agrees, and she becomes upset. He explains that he is overtired and in a state of extreme tension, caused by the strain of his business. Originally, in order to get away alone with Paul, Babbitt had planned to tell Myra that he had to go to New York to see a client; now he breaks down and blurts out the truth: he and Paul are going to spend part of their vacation without their wives in order to calm their frayed nerves. As Paul had predicted, Myra is unable to understand this notion, but at last she consents and promises to help convince Zilla Riesling that their husbands are doing what is best for them. She also does her best to comfort Babbitt because the strain of confession has badly upset him. Babbitt is put to bed by his wife and as he lies waiting for sleep to envelop him, he suddenly realizes that he has gained freedom. But this curious and unexpected thought only makes him more uncomfortable.

Commentary

After Lewis shows us A Typical Day in the Life of George F. Babbitt, he now focuses on one of the favorite targets of America's satirists: the American cocktail-dinner party. George and Myra Babbitt give a party for twelve people, and it is, Lewis says, one of the "great events" of Babbitt's spring. Lewis, however, intends for this section of the novel to be more than just an excuse for him to laugh at Americans trying to be very clever and important; he uses this party to bring to a crisis some of the discontent that we have seen festering within Babbitt.

After the guests have gone home and Myra has given Babbitt permission to go early to the Maine woods with Paul, Babbitt is faced, for the first time in his life, with an entirely new challenge: freedom. His frustrated longing to escape has been gratified, and he has never been so frightened.

Lewis prepares us for Babbitt's emotional crisis in three steps: first, he shows us Babbitt's solid citizen self reduced to a bumbling Mr. Milquetoast as he begs liquor from the bootlegger; then he shows us Babbitt restoring his self-image as he gloats over his cache of liquor; later, Babbitt's sense of importance expands as he sips the cocktails, greets his guests, and plays host. Then his self-esteem shrivels: too much rich food and liquor sicken him, and his ache of discontent returns. Very simply, Babbitt is a man of routine, and today his routine has been violated. First, there was the humiliation at the bootlegger's; then, during the evening, there was the strain of being a host. The veneer of the hearty, hale-fellow solid citizen begins to crack and, at the chapter's end, we watch a frightened Babbitt trying to hide in sleep.

Returning to the party scene, note that Lewis is showing us that in addition to being hypocrites, the Babbitts are also bigots. Babbitt prides himself on being a "compassionate" conservative; his friends include an intellectual and a poet; that is, Babbitt has intellectual and poetic friends – but only if they dress like regular folks, make money, and are inoffensive. Babbitt is pleased that his party will include Howard Littlefield, Ph.D., and Chum Frink, poet. Babbitt's wife is not pleased, however, that the party includes the owner of a mere laundry.

Lewis also mocks Prohibition in this chapter, calling it the "reign of righteousness," and showing us how degrading Prohibition was when an ordinary businessman, such as Babbitt, wanted to buy a bottle of liquor. Babbitt must leave the safe districts of Uptown, drive through the narrow, tenement-and-brothel-lined streets of The Arbor, carrying the guilt of a criminal. He realizes that his $125 suit carries no clout, and note that he uses a forced, uncertain speech with the bootlegger. Lewis has Babbitt "stalk plumply" up to the bar, follow the bartender "as delicately as a cat," then pay more than the value of the liquor. Babbitt seems unbearably uncomfortable, but Lewis shows us Babbitt's even further discomfort in an entirely different kind of establishment – when he stops at the blue, frilly Vecchia's for ice cream. These two scenes – where Babbitt was supposed to perform a "man's work" for the party – contrast significantly and work together beautifully to aggravate Babbitt's temper just prior to the actual party.

At last, Lewis serves up The Party for us; and, with the aid of silk socks and silver studs, he transforms Babbitt again. Lewis uses satire so effectively because no one before him had mined this rich vein of Americana. Lewis was a pioneer in mimicking American mores and, for that reason, his cocktail party may seem overdone today, yet the Babbitts' party is a very different sort of party from the kind of cocktail party satirized today. The men at Babbitt's party roar, guffaw, josh broadly, and say, "Oh, gosh"; they call cocktails "breaking the law a little"; their giggling wives dutifully refuse a second drink. These men have worked hard, made money, and silently pride themselves on their hard-earned eliteness; after a few drinks, they pride themselves aloud. The masses of shiftless workmen, they say, need Prohibition, but as far as they themselves are concerned, Prohibition is an invasion of "personal liberty." They say this with booming profundity, while Lewis points all the while to their coarse manners, their smutty jokes, and their fumbling attempts at flirting with one another's wives.

As the liquor-warmed gaiety wears thin, Lewis leaves the various guests and concentrates on the metamorphosis that is taking place within Babbitt. Never before has Babbitt admitted to himself that he is bored by his friends, but tonight he has taken too big a dose of food and friends. He is overpowered and an easy prey for "the curst discontent." It is no wonder that after the party Babbitt dissolves in tears. In a way, we understand. Lewis has made Babbitt's friends so sickeningly smug and Babbitt's home situation so barren of warm, personal love that almost anyone would break down.

CHAPTER 10

Summary

One evening, Babbitt and his wife visit the Rieslings in their modern apartment. They spend an enjoyable few hours until Zilla begins her usual complaints about Paul, criticizing and nagging him until he becomes nasty. The Babbitts try to patch matters up, but have no success. At last, Babbitt can stand it no longer. Rising to his feet, he shouts a series of denunciations at Zilla, causing her to break into tears. He demands that Zilla allow Paul to go to Maine with him, and she sobbingly agrees. She begs Babbitt to understand that she is sorry, that she means no harm, and that she will try to be a better wife in the future.

On the way home, Myra accuses Babbitt of bullying Zilla and suggests that his only motive for doing so was to feel noble and self-righteous. Babbitt denies the charge, but later he realizes that Myra may have been right. The thought troubles him for awhile, but he finally decides that his over-sensitivity is due to his nervousness. After the trip to Maine, both he and Paul will be emotionally healthier.

Like two excited young boys, Babbitt and Riesling purchase all their fishing and camping equipment, and after a few more days, they begin their journey. They board the New York Express and ride in the smoking car with a number of other businessmen. Paul remains aloof and spends most of his time reading; Babbitt, however, has a rousing, satisfying time with some newly-met cronies, discussing politics, business problems, and telling off-color jokes.

Commentary

This chapter contains another of Lewis' sharp-edged portraits of smart, modern living, here exemplified by the Rieslings' apartment. The hidden sink, the hidden refrigerator, and the hidden bed are all caricatured. But the tone of the satire changes as soon as Zilla Riesling begins speaking. Bleached and rigidly corseted, Zilla Riesling shrieks, gibbers, and howls. She bays; her voice is a "dagger of corroded brass." She revels in ridiculing her husband's quietness; she is "vicious in the name of virtue," and she wallows in melodramatic, egotistical shame after Babbitt chastises her.

In contrast, Paul Riesling is a quiet man, rubbing his fingers and twitching his hands; Mrs. Babbitt is maternal, fussy but placid, and she condemns her avenging husband for his outburst; and Babbitt himself is smug about his success in taming the shrew. We enjoy watching Zilla receive Babbitt's tongue-lashing; it is a perfect punishment for her, and it does not matter that she is neurotically enjoying Babbitt's upbraiding; she is getting exactly what she deserves. Yet the feeling that justice is being meted out is destroyed when Babbitt, scolded by Myra, begins to doubt his own actions. He sulks, he is outraged; then, excusing his actions on the grounds of fatigue, he makes a final effort at speaking the truth: he did it for his friend Paul.

Ending Chapter 10, Lewis zeroes in on the man's world. The man's world, according to literary cliche, is one of rough, potent virility; in this chapter, however, the man's world is a smoking car. Babbitt and the men whom he talks with in the car become, under Lewis' pen, big men, the "council"; they give "verdicts" and nod "sagely." Babbitt and his friends seem quite serious about their newfound fraternity, but it is not a man's seriousness; it is the seriousness of little boys bragging to one another. These men, like Babbitt, are Lewis' satirical targets, his representatives of the American middle-class male, displaying all the bad qualities of their social group; they are patriotic to the point of being chauvinistic, poorly educated, materialistic, intolerant, and conformist in all their ideas. Basically, they have never bothered to examine or evaluate any of their beliefs, but they are supremely self-confident and sanctimonious in their ignorance.

CHAPTERS 11-12

Summary

Babbitt and Paul spend a few hours in New York between trains. They visit the Pennsylvania Hotel, the city's newest, because Babbitt, as a realtor, is interested in seeing it. Afterward, at Paul's suggestion, they go to the docks to see an ocean liner. Babbitt is impressed by the majestic vessel and expresses a sudden desire to see Europe, but he is not serious. Paul, on the other hand, is strangely silent.

The two men continue their trip and eventually arrive at their destination – Lake Sunasquam, in the mountains of Maine. They hasten to change into their camping clothes and demonstrate their independence by openly using the chewing tobacco that both their wives consider vulgar.

The next week is spent sleeping late, fishing, boating, and hiking. At night they stay up late, drinking and playing poker with the Indian guides. As the days pass, much of their tension and nervous talkativeness – byproducts of life in Zenith – disappear. They become quieter and more relaxed, and they fall back into the closeness and mutual understanding of their college days.

As the time draws near for their wives to arrive, Babbitt begins to get restless. Paul, however, has made resolutions and plans to try to live harmoniously with Zilla. When the wives appear, they both insist that the "boys" continue their "activities," and, indeed on the first two nights, Babbitt does stay out and play cards, but soon both he and Paul return to the routine of being married men again.

After two more weeks, they all prepare to return to Zenith. The relaxed living and fresh air have done a lot to calm Babbitt and make him feel healthier. He is not eager to leave the mountains and go back to the office, but he is full of confidence and anticipates a great year.

On the trip home, full of new assurance, Babbitt vows to give up smoking again, but his determination lasts no longer than it ever has. Within a few days, the busy regimen of his office prevents him from even remembering his resolution.

After returning to Zenith, Babbitt decides to expand his recreational activities. He is an ardent baseball fan and vows to deepen this interest by attending three games a week. Despite his love of baseball, however, he is unable to find the time after the first week.

Every Saturday, Babbitt plays golf at his country club and finds that the game is a source of relaxation and healthy exercise for him, and one evening each week, Babbitt, his wife, and Tinka go to the movies. Babbitt particularly enjoys three kinds of films – those with pretty girls in bathing suits, those with policemen or cowboys and lots of shooting, and those with slapstick comedians. Myra prefers society romances set in New York or London. Besides baseball, golf, and the movies, Babbitt's other recreational activities include bridge, long auto drives, and conversations with Paul.

Commentary

Paul Riesling tries to be a regular guy; he tries to say friendly things to other men, but somehow he never sounds "friendly." Either he is too spontaneous or he is too reserved. Babbitt tries to help; he tries to bolster and cheer Paul, but Paul does not have Babbitt's capacity of really enjoying off-color stories nor does he enjoy bragging. Paul's values are not Babbitt's and at no time is this difference more evident than during Paul and Babbitt's sightseeing in New York. Of all the things they do and plan to see in New York, Babbitt wants to see the Pennsylvania Hotel. For Babbitt, it is the only thing worthwhile for strangers to see because it is America's biggest hotel. But Babbitt does not marvel at its magnificence; instead, he marvels at the number of dollars that the hotel must surely gross every day. A true materialist, Babbitt is awed by the amount of money involved.

Paul, on the other hand, wants to go down to the docks and see an ocean liner. To him, the floating ship is a symbol of escape, something which is capable of taking him away from his nagging wife and his boring, if successful, business. Babbitt is too insensitive to realize that Paul is emotionally overwhelmed by the possibility of sailing away and leaving his unhappy life behind him.

In contrast to Paul, who certainly does not "need" Zilla's nagging, Babbitt "needs" Myra's nagging because it is constant and secure. Myra may be a fat and unattractive component of Babbitt's life, but foremost she is a stabilizer and a source of great strength. When Myra appears at the camp, Babbitt automatically takes himself to task: he has been lazy and he is anxious for familiar things and familiar routines. He wonders about his business: is it able to function without him? He takes himself in hand as though he were lecturing an errant friend; he sells himself on his coming success in the new year. This runaway trip to the Maine woods has accomplished the re-birth of a salesman.

While relating Babbitt's reorganization of priorities, Lewis tells us in an aside that he thinks that America's love of baseball is actually just a cover, a sublimation for the country's homicidal instincts. And later, in other asides, he attacks more examples of standard Americana—for example, the American habit of doing things at top speed. Lewis believes that Americans eat too fast, work too fast, and talk too fast—in order to make more money. Americans join country clubs and play golf, as Babbitt does, not because they enjoy them, but because it is expected and because it is part of being a solid citizen, a social American.

Often, satirists of Middle America assume that merely because one is a member of a country club and lives in a ranch-style house in the suburbs that one's life is automatically sterile and meaningless. Lewis is making such sweeping generalizations here, and one should avoid being converted too quickly to Lewis' too-narrow perspective. There are flaws in America and there are flaws in Babbitt himself, but one cannot take Lewis' view of Babbitt as *the* testament of truth about America. One should approach this novel as Sinclair Lewis' testament about America.

CHAPTERS 13–14

Summary

Babbitt, like all his business colleagues, is a member of the State Association of Real Estate Boards. The annual convention of this organization is to be held in the city of Monarch this year, and Babbitt is selected to be one of Zenith's delegates. While meeting with Cecil Rountree, the delegation chairman, Babbitt repeats his favorite ideas about real estate's being a profession with the same dignity as medicine or law. Rountree is impressed and invites Babbitt to read a paper on the subject at the convention.

For the next few days, Babbitt spends all his spare time working on his speech, making his family miserable with his intense concentration. He makes no progress at all until one night when he decides to ignore what little he knows about style, form, order, and other rhetorical rules. He writes down what he feels – just as it occurs to him – and in a short time, the speech is complete.

The Zenith delegation leaves for the convention with all the noise and fanfare that is typical of such affairs. On the train and later at the meeting itself, there is a wide variety of horseplay – with costumes, placards, and much friendly rivalry between representatives of different cities. Babbitt delivers a stirring speech on the nobility and responsibility of the realtor's profession, and he suddenly finds that he has become one of the most popular and well-known figures at the convention. Everyone seeks his acquaintance, and he is appointed to an important committee. The next day, the convention ends and most of the delegates go home.

Babbitt and several friends decide to stay in Monarch for an additional night of fun and good fellowship. They spend a few hours playing cards and drinking heavily; then after a good dinner, they attend a burlesque theater and a night club. By this time, most of the men have little self-control or discretion left and are eager to cut loose in a way they cannot do at home. The tipsy group decides to visit a red-light district. Babbitt is terrified by the idea and tries to escape from the taxi, but he realizes that he actually wants to go to a whorehouse. He joins the other men, loudly proclaiming that Zenith has "got more houses and hootch-parlors . . . than any burg in the state."

The next morning Babbitt, like the others, has a terrible hangover; he returns to Zenith and tells no one of his late-night escapade. Before long, Babbitt has almost forgotten the night of debauchery.

In the autumn, election time comes around. Seneca Doane, the radical attorney, is a candidate for mayor, running on a pro-labor platform. The Democrats and Republicans join forces to support Lucas Prout, a wealthy and respectable manufacturer. Prout is also supported by the banks, the newspapers, the Chamber of Commerce, and all the reputable businessmen in the city.

Babbitt is the precinct leader in Floral Heights, but there is no contest in this solid district, and he desires a more challenging assignment. He volunteers his services as an orator for the Prout campaign. Before long, he is one of Prout's most active supporters, making speeches and conducting meetings every night in Zenith's working-class neighborhoods. Babbitt's name appears in the newspapers several times during the campaign, and he begins to develop an impressive reputation. He enjoys his new role immensely.

When Prout is elected, Babbitt is one of nineteen speakers at the victory banquet. He is rewarded for his campaign work by being given secret advance information about the extension of paved highways in the city. This will be of great value to him in the real-estate business.

Later that year, Babbitt delivers the key address at the annual dinner of the Zenith Real Estate Board. In his speech, he praises Zenith as a jewel among American cities, and he extols at great length the standardized, middle-class American way of life. In addition, he attacks socialism, "long-haired" liberalism and intellectualism, and all the college professors and writers who have the audacity to question the long-held beliefs of people like himself and his audience.

The speech is reprinted in the *Advocate-Times* and is well received. Babbitt continues to make additional orations on a number of subjects, in and around Zenith. He is frequently mentioned in the newspapers. Even Vergil Gunch, an already well-known local speaker, compliments Babbitt on his speechmaking abilities.

Commentary

For a long time, Babbitt has lived quietly and securely on Zenith's upper-middle-class plateau. Now, however, he is about to lose his anonymous solid citizen image; he is about to become a name and a face in the Zenith newspapers. Ironically, this sudden local fame does not come from Babbitt's usually shrewd business acumen; instead, it comes by chance and with Cecil Rountree's help. Heretofore, Babbitt has never valued Rountree's snobbish ways, but Babbitt's attitude changes after he is offered the chance to speak to the State Association of Real Estate Boards—and Babbitt's destiny changes.

Accepting the offer to give a speech is easy enough, but writing the speech is another matter for Babbitt. Lewis calls Babbitt's writing of the speech an "event," and he characterizes Babbitt as a comic, dictatorial bully preparing for the creative act of writing. A special notebook is bought and the family is cowed to silence while Babbitt, looking important, tries in vain to compose a fitting oration. Finally, he simply writes down his own ideas, and the speech is finished.

After Lewis shows us Babbitt the creative thinker, he shows us Babbitt the super patriot. Babbitt is loud and ridiculous, and his apparent love for his country and for Zenith proves only one thing: Babbitt is vulgar about his patriotism. He rumbles, swells, gloats, and is lordly and distasteful.

However, Babbitt is not unique; at the convention we see that Babbittism abounds. Suddenly we are in a sea of Babbitts, men who exhort brotherly love, but not at the cost of their fierce hometown partianship. The cities of Monarch, Sparta, Zenith, and others are deadly competitive. The real-estate convention is really a collection of jealous city organizations, using the convention as an excuse to show off to one another and as an excuse for a day or two of middling debauchery. There is an atmosphere of carnival and the spirit of Babbitt is its king.

After Babbitt's speech, he becomes "Brother Babbitt," and "George" to people he doesn't even know. From solid citizen, Babbitt becomes important citizen; he is playfully frisky with Mrs. Sassburger, swigs bootleg whiskey surreptitiously from a coffee cup, then goes to a burlesque show. Babbitt is gorging himself on the first taste of celebrity status.

Clearly, Lewis is now chronicling the adventures of George F. Babbitt, public speaker. Speaking in behalf of the bankers and the Zenith Chamber of Commerce, Babbitt convinces many crowds of workmen that Seneca Doane's sympathies are *not* with labor, as claimed, and that the real hero of the working man is Lucas Prout. Babbitt has a knack for being likable, and he capitalizes on it. He believes that he is doing what is best for Zenith because, according to Lewis, he "almost" likes the common worker and therefore speaks to him in "all candor, honesty, and sincerity."

Actually, all three qualities are similar – but Babbitt, when he parades them as evidence of his goodwill, makes himself appear three times as generous to his audience. He poses before them as a man blessed with poverty, a man who is condemned because of innate brilliance to be steward to America's financial complexities.

Note here that Babbitt's patriotic platitudes are full of hate – hate that is born from the fear of anything foreign, anything different. Babbitt's friends oppose the working man; Zenith opposes its neighboring towns; Babbitt's America opposes other nations. Yet they all call for – they pray and plead for – brotherhood, love, and solidarity. In other words, if anyone would criticize America he would be, to Babbitt, suspect and a traitor by definition. Babbitt is not preaching compassion for either America or for other men; he is wooing fear and hatred.

CHAPTER 15

Summary

Although he is now a prominent citizen, Babbitt is not fully satisfied, for he has not received the social recognition which he feels he and his family deserve. He looks forward to his university class dinner since he will have an opportunity to mingle with such Zenith aristocrats as Charlie McKelvey, the millionaire contractor, Irving Tate, the tool manufacturer, and Adelbert Dobson, the fashionable interior decorator. In theory, these men are all his friends because they attended college together, and they are still on a first-name basis, despite the fact that Babbitt is never invited to their homes.

The banquet is held in a private room at the Union Club, and although Babbitt is dressed and groomed properly, he enters these sacred precincts with nervous awe. Gathered in the room are some sixty people. The successful ones (like Babbitt) wear evening clothes, while the others are dressed in their best business suits. The different outfits soon divide the men into two groups.

With Paul following, Babbitt seeks out the company of Charlie McKelvey, and later he sits alongside the millionaire when they eat. The former friends seemingly enjoy recalling their college pranks and discussing business. Babbitt invites McKelvey to his house, and Charlie vaguely agrees that he will come sometime. To Babbitt, this is as good as a definite promise, and his spirits rise as he visualizes himself entering Zenith's most fashionable circles.

Early in December, the Babbitts ask the McKelveys to dinner. After changing the date several times, the McKelveys actually do arrive for dinner. Naturally, Babbitt and his wife are very excited about this opportunity to impress the monied McKelveys. They also invite a prominent physician and a well-known attorney and their wives, hoping that such admirable guests will impress the McKelveys. Babbitt's chest swells with pride as the McKelveys drive up only fifteen minutes late in their chauffeured limousine. Although Babbitt and his wife are on their best behavior, the McKelveys are obviously bored and leave early after making a poor excuse. Myra tries to hide her sorrow, and Babbitt attempts to comfort her. Finally, Myra cries herself to sleep. During the next few weeks, the Babbitts eagerly await a return invitation from the McKelveys, but it never arrives.

At the reunion dinner, Babbitt also greeted Ed Overbrook, another classmate. Overbrook has been a failure since leaving school, and he presently operates a small insurance business. Overbrook and his large family live in an old house in an unfashionable section of Zenith. Ed reacts to Babbitt in much the same way that Babbitt did to McKelvey. He evidently believes that through Babbitt, he and his wife will be able to advance their social status. The Overbrooks invite the Babbitts to dinner, and after changing the date and putting the dinner party off, the Babbitts finally accept. At dinner, Babbitt and his wife unwittingly behave toward the Overbrooks and their friends in the same condescending way that the McKelveys behaved toward the Babbitts. In this case, the Babbitts arrive late and leave early, after unsuccessfully hiding their boredom and making lame excuses and vague promises.

For a time, the Babbitts consider inviting the Overbrooks to their house in return. They never do, however, feeling that the Overbrooks would be an embarrassment in front of their own friends and, besides that, the poorer couple would probably be ill at ease in the Babbitts' company. The Babbitts never realize that this is precisely the way that the McKelveys feel about the Babbitts. Shortly thereafter, Babbitt and his wife forget about the Overbrooks.

Commentary

The mood in this chapter, instead of being bitterly sarcastic, is softer and more comic. Lewis structures the scene in this way: first, the Babbitts idolize and cater to the very successful McKelveys, then are snubbed by them. Later, the Babbitts are idolized and catered to by the not-quite-so-successful Overbrooks, who are snubbed by the Babbitts. The lesson is clear: the so-called classless American democracy is really made up of several territorial strata, and each social class jealousy guards its boundaries from interlopers.

At the class reunion, Babbitt stays close to the heels of Charles McKelvey (a great success in big business and a former Big Man on Campus). He hangs onto McKelvey's every word while noting how the failures of the class all look enviously at him (Babbitt). He doesn't recognize the parallel in adulation, but we do. And we also note that when the Babbitts dismally entertain the Overbrooks that the Overbrooks say the same wrong things to the Babbitts, the same kind of things that the Babbitts said earlier to the McKelveys.

For example, during dinner, Overbrook praises Babbitt, just as Babbitt praised the McKelveys; Babbitt is asked what New York and Chicago are really like, and in the same way, Babbitt asked Lucille McKelvey about Europe. In both cases, both Babbitt and Lucille reply that their interest in these cities is food—not culture—as their questioner supposed. Thus, as the long, tedious dinners are finished, Lewis tells us that the McKelveys did not speak of the Babbitts again and that the Babbitts did not speak of the Overbrooks again.

CHAPTERS 16-17

Summary

Babbitt is unhappy that the McKelveys and their circle have not accepted him. In reaction to this snub, he strives even harder to become an even more prominent citizen. He continues to make speeches on important issues whenever the opportunity arises, and he is active in the Elks and other organizations to which he belongs. Babbitt is a member of one of Zenith's largest and richest churches – Chatham Road Presbyterian. The eloquent and efficient pastor, the Reverend Doctor John Jennison Drew, is highly esteemed and respected by all the better people of the city. Reverend Drew is intelligent and amiable; he is a staunch defender of business and an advocate of modern, manly Christianity.

One Sunday, after a particularly inspiring service, Dr. Drew has a private conference with Babbitt, Chum Frink, and William W. Eathorne, president of the First State Bank of Zenith, and the seventy-one-year-old scion of one of the city's wealthiest and most ancient families. The pastor explains to the three men that he wants them to form a committee to devise ways to enlarge the Sunday School attendance and gain increased publicity for the church.

Babbitt agrees to help, although he is the sort of man who has never bothered to think much about religion. Babbitt believes that churchgoing is a highly respectable activity to engage in and that it is good for prospective customers to see that he is an active churchgoer. He usually understands very little in the poetic and complicated sermons of Dr. Drew, but he feels that, in some mystical way, listening to them will do him good and draw him nearer to God.

As a member of the Sunday School Advisory Committee, Babbitt spends several weeks observing the classes and examining the textbooks. He finds everything very sincere, very devout, and very dull. After reaching this conclusion, he spends a few evenings at home reading Sunday School journals and church magazines. He is deeply impressed by the intelligent and businesslike attitude toward Christianity which these publications demonstrate. Babbitt resolves to take an active part in the affairs of his church.

One afternoon, there is a committee meeting in the imposing Eathorne mansion. Babbitt and Frink attend with an air of awe, for outsiders are rarely invited to this house. Eathorne outlines his ideas for the advancement of the Sunday School. Babbitt disagrees with him, however, and tactfully suggests his own program for church school improvement. Babbitt's system takes advantage of all the latest innovations in public relations and advertising. His ideas include the introduction of contests and a number of other educational novelties. Most of these promise to be effective in increasing attendance, although they have little to do with religion and might seem even a bit irreverent to some people. Eathorne turns out to be less conservative than Babbitt had suspected and enthusiastically agrees to the program. After the meeting ends, Babbitt takes a long drive home, exulting privately over his triumph.

Following Babbitt's advice, Kenneth Escott, a young reporter on the *Advocate-Times,* is secretly hired as part-time press agent for the church. Not long afterward, articles praising Chatham Road Presbyterian and Dr. Drew begin to appear in all the city's newspapers. Babbitt's program is adopted in full by the Sunday School. Before long, attendance has leaped from fourth largest in the city to second largest. The pastor and all the members are very pleased with Babbitt's achievement.

Babbitt brings Escott home for dinner once or twice, and the young reporter and Verona quickly become good friends; they share the same concern for "culture" and "serious ideas" and are both "sensible radicals." In order to please Babbitt, Escott continues arranging for Dr. Drew to get favorable publicity.

After awhile, the pastor arranges a small dinner for the members of the Sunday School committee. Babbitt uses this opportunity to strengthen his acquaintance with Eathorne. Some months later, he takes advantage of this new friendship by taking out a private loan from Eathorne's bank in order to finance a dishonest and clandestine real-estate deal he is involved in. He and Eathorne both make a nice profit from this transaction. Babbitt continues to attend church whenever it is convenient, and he loudly announces to his family and friends that there is no better place to make respectable and profitable acquaintances than in church.

Commentary

Without a doubt, Babbitt's name is becoming well-known in Zenith and, probably more important, in his own estimation. A successful business, the right kind of home, and the right kind of wife and children used to be Babbitt's goals – but he attained them. Now his horizons are expanding: Babbitt is on the verge of becoming just the merest shadow of the orator that he once hoped to become. Also, he is checking the daily editorials less frequently and Howard Littlefield's opinions aren't as important as they used to be. However, Babbitt is not independent of Littlefield or newspaper editorial; he has been nurtured on them, and he is, in a large sense, a product of newspaper editorials and Howard Littlefield's opinions.

At this point, Lewis takes us backstage, behind Babbitt's newfound rhetorical brilliance and exposes the same old Babbitt for us. Babbitt's church affiliation is, as we might expect, with a church that is both wealthy and manly. Babbitt's pastor denounces labor unions, just as Babbitt does, and he confides to Babbitt, with humble pride, just as Babbitt does to selected people, that he too was once a poor boy. Naturally, Babbitt is sympathetic to such seemingly humble honesty.

Babbitt is given a chance to hobnob with W. W. Eathorne, the quintessential symbol of Zenith's Old Money. This kind of money is best of all; it is far better than Charles McKelvey's money, which is Zenith's New Money. Babbitt swells with happiness as he accepts Dr. Drew's offer to help Frink and Eathorne make their Sunday School attendance Number One. Babbitt is in his element: while his theology is vague, he does know buying and selling. A Sunday School record attendance is just that: a matter of buying and selling. Selling God is just another challenging merchandising problem to solve.

CHAPTER 18

Summary

Babbitt always sees his children several times each day, but aside from his concern about their expenditures, he never pays much attention to them. Now, however, Kenneth Escott's attentions to Verona arouse his interest. Babbitt also starts to worry about Ted. His son is a good athlete and mechanic and is involved in all the social activities of his high school, but his academic grades are low. Furthermore, Ted seems opposed to attending college or law school; even worse, the boy is evidently very fond of Eunice Littlefield. Babbitt likes the girl – he has known her since she was a child – but he considers her flighty and immature. Her greatest ambition is to become a movie star.

44

Toward the end of his senior year, Ted has a party at home for his classmates. Babbitt and Myra try to be helpful, but they soon learn that the youngsters do not appreciate their efforts. In addition, Babbitt is scandalized to discover that the teenagers drink and smoke and behave in what he feels is an unhealthy "adult manner." Howard Littlefield, Eunice's father, drops in on the party for awhile, and he is as shocked as Babbitt. He takes his daughter home.

Babbitt's family problems increase when Myra's parents sell their house and move to a downtown hotel; now, every week or so, Babbitt has to spend a dull evening with them because they are lonely. Babbitt's mother, who still lives in the rural up-state village of Catawba, where he was born, decides to visit Zenith. She stays at his house for nearly a month and constantly embarrasses him by telling stories about his childhood and his dead father. Shortly afterward, Martin, Babbitt's half-brother, brings his family for a short visit. Babbitt dislikes Martin, but forces himself to be nice for their mother's sake. Martin is rude and surly, and his behavior makes Babbitt's effort more difficult. All of these incidents increase Babbitt's discontent with life.

Babbitt is ill for awhile in February, but soon learns to enjoy the solitude and attention of being in a sick bed. He reviews his affairs while recovering. He is dissatisfied, but as soon as he is well again, he returns to his old routines.

Commentary

In this chapter, Lewis draws a portrait of Babbitt as a man growing old. Babbitt doesn't understand why Ted isn't bursting with pep and ambition, why Ted's grades are not top-rate, or why Ted dates Eunice Littlefield. Babbitt doesn't understand bobbed hair, short skirts, rolled stockings, or women who smoke. His heroes and goals are not his children's. Even more disturbing is the fact that he is treated like an old man, just when he has discovered a new and rejuvenated self. His eyes still delight in such pretty young things as Eunice Littlefield, yet he is treated like an "older man."

The truth is that Babbitt's children are no longer children. Babbitt was not able to afford cigarettes in silver cases when he was their age, yet he has made enough money so that Ted can use silver cigarette cases; understandably, Babbitt envies his son's youth and its luxuries. Ted's girlfriends are prettier than Babbitt's were; Babbitt's girlfriends were plain and demure and uninteresting. Today, girls enjoy being attractive. Babbitt feels that he is an anachronism. He feels young, yet the young treat him old. And the old? Babbitt's mother reminisces about her "Georgie" and treats Babbitt as though he were still her baby. Yet Babbitt is not a baby. He is not a boy, and he is not old. But Babbitt is no longer young, and the discovery is painful.

CHAPTERS 19-20

Summary

The real-estate deal involving options on land required by the Street Traction Company for repair shops finally comes through. Babbitt makes a profit of $3,000 and several officials of the company do equally well. About the same time, a customer complains that Stanley Graff has cheated him, and Babbitt fires the salesman. He lectures Graff sternly on ethics and honesty, but Graff refuses to listen politely to Babbitt's pious moralizing. He vents all his accumulated anger at his former employer. Babbitt indignantly threatens to have Graff arrested for cheating, but the salesman warns Babbitt that he will disclose all he knows about Babbitt's part in the recently completed, corrupt Street Traction deal. Graff leaves, and Babbitt decides not to take any further action.

Babbitt makes a business trip to Chicago and takes Ted along. The two of them go to the theater and the best restaurants and have a wonderful time. Their relationship becomes closer, and Babbitt realizes that his son is an adult. He begins to refer proudly to himself and Ted as "the Babbitt men."

After Ted leaves, Babbitt encounters Sir Gerald Doak, an English industrialist who was entertained by the McKelveys and their circle during his recent visit to Zenith. Babbitt read about these events in the newspaper and resented not receiving an invitation to any of the parties or banquets. The two businessmen quickly become friends, for they share many of the same conservative views and enjoy the same sort of amusements. Babbitt is astonished to learn that Doak dislikes "high society" and that he prefers going to cowboy movies.

One evening, by chance, Babbitt encounters Paul Riesling in a Chicago restaurant. Paul is accompanied by a rather frowsy looking middle-aged woman and is annoyed at meeting Babbitt because Zilla and everyone else in Zenith think that he is in Akron on business. He tells Babbitt that he will see him later that night.

Babbitt goes to Paul's hotel room, and the two old friends spend several hours talking. Paul confides that his life with Zilla has become unbearable and that he is intimate with another woman, May Arnold. May is a widow, and Paul claims that she offers him the understanding and affection that he cannot get from his wife. He frequently comes to Chicago to see May. Babbitt starts preaching to Paul about moral obligations, but finally relents and agrees to stick by his friend no matter what happens. In Zenith, Paul rarely touches alcohol, but now he is drinking heavily. Later, when Babbitt is alone, he thinks about Paul and cries.

Back in Zenith, Babbitt goes to see Zilla in order to borrow something for his wife. While there, the topic of Paul comes up casually, as he had planned. Zilla suspects that her husband is seeing another woman, but Babbitt denies this notion. She discusses her marital problems with Babbitt and admits that she is cruel and insensitive to Paul's needs. She promises to be a better wife in the future.

After Paul returns, he tells Babbitt that his wife is being a lot nicer, but that it is too late. Her old ways continue to surface now and then, and he has already learned to detest her. Some day, he says, he will find a way to get rid of her.

Commentary

Babbitt's real-estate business is a success because Babbitt is clever – and because, if sanctioned by precedent, Babbitt will go to any practical lengths to make a dollar. He does this kind of finagling regularly. He has his own intelligence network that tells him which tracts of land are soon to become valuable so that he can, very quietly, buy them up. He has secret associates and makes secret deals. But he does all this in the name of good business sense.

There is, however, one thing that Babbitt will not tolerate in the name of good business: an employee who makes his own shifty deals. Babbitt, therefore, in the name of righteousness, fires Stanley Graff and, of course, this act is supremely ironic – a fact which Graff recognizes. He, and we, enjoy Babbitt's discomfort when Babbitt must attempt, politely, to discharge Graff. Graff smirks at Babbitt's hypocrisy. He insults Babbitt – and Babbitt's children – and threatens to expose Babbitt. Naturally, Babbitt is terrified. But we suspect that Graff's lecture does no more than frighten Babbitt temporarily because Babbitt knows that ultimately he, Babbitt, is the boss; he has elitist privileges. He and his Booster friends have an automatic, built-in, double set of values: one for themselves and one for their workers.

After Ted returns to Zenith, leaving Babbitt alone in Chicago, Babbitt is empty and deflated until he accidentally meets Sir Gerald Doak. Doak, like McKelvey and Eathorne, is "royalty" to Babbitt; yet Doak proves himself to be even more. Sir Gerald enjoys Babbitt's stories and liquor because he detests all of America's "social rot," especially all of the American hosting which he has had to endure. Babbitt enjoys Sir Gerald because in Sir Gerald's company, Babbitt can secretly indulge himself in "social rot."

Babbitt seems happy, but, as usual, Lewis is busy undermining Babbitt's groundswell of happiness. This time, Babbitt's good spirits are shattered when he sees Paul Riesling having dinner with a dilapidated-looking woman. Why should this upset Babbitt – especially since he knows that Paul has joked about extramarital affairs before? Babbitt is upset because Paul is breaking the rules. It's one thing to be with the boys, implying certain lusty nighttime adventures, but it's another thing to flaunt a flabby, over-rouged woman of forty in public. In other words, in Babbitt's code, the rule is: brag about it, but don't actually do it, and if you *must* do it, don't *ever* do it in public.

Babbitt's reaction is surprising. Possibly Lewis overdraws this scene. Even Babbitt knows that he's acting like a fool, but Paul has done something that is in very bad taste, and Babbitt fears that some terrible, ultimate disgrace may happen. Paul is undergoing a crisis, the woman is a symptom of that crisis, and thus we see how Babbitt reacts to his best friend in a time of crisis: he is more concerned about Paul's position in the community than he is about Paul. He is dismayed that Paul would actually have sex with another woman and tell her about his troubles with Zilla – troubles that no one but Babbitt should hear. To Babbitt, a man doesn't confess to just anyone that his wife is driving him crazy. Babbitt is no longer Paul's only confidant.

CHAPTER 21

Summary

Babbitt is an active member of the Zenith Boosters' Club, the local chapter of a businessman's organization with thousands of branches in the United States and several foreign countries. At the second weekly club luncheon in March, the annual election of officers is held. To Babbitt's great surprise and joy, he is elected vice-president.

That same day, he receives horrifying news. Paul has shot Zilla; he is in jail and she is in the hospital.

Commentary

This is our first look at the workings of the Boosters' Club that we have heard so much about, but Lewis does not linger unduly over its inanities. He has more important matters to investigate, and he uses the Boosters' Club scene primarily to show us the greatest moment (thus far) in Babbitt's life: Babbitt's being elected vice-president of the organization. Certainly, Babbitt is not being honored without cause. If anyone were entitled to the office, it would seem to be George F. Babbitt. He exudes optimism, ready pleasantries, and good business sense. People like his store of positive-thinking platitudes, the platitudes he has used for years to insulate himself from unhappy reflection. In fact, Babbitt has encased himself in so many layers of these banal platitudes that he has almost successfully protected himself from all anxiety and despondency.

Meanwhile, Chum Frink is using his high-pressure tactics on the club, selling them on the financial, rather than the aesthetic advantages of forming a symphony orchestra. Babbitt is being nominated, seconded, and declared vice president, when – suddenly – Paul Riesling shoots his wife. While Babbitt is reveling at the peak of his professional success, his best friend commits an act that is un-optimistic, un-manly, un-pleasant, and not good for business.

CHAPTERS 22–23

Summary

Babbitt is able to see Paul at the City Prison only after using his influence with Mayor Prout. He visits Riesling in his cell, and Paul antagonistically expects Babbitt to be moralistic, but Babbitt says that he wants only to help. Paul is terribly upset and expresses remorse for his crime. He hopes that Zilla will not die, and Babbitt tries to comfort him.

For the rest of the day, Babbitt is very sad and confused. He forbids his family to discuss the case because wherever he goes, he hears or imagines the gossip and scandal-mongering, and he wants a little peace. The next afternoon, however, Babbitt discovers that he is afraid to face his friends at the Athletic Club. When he comes in for lunch, though, the men demonstrate an understanding of his feelings and no one mentions the matter. Babbitt's gratitude to them is sincere.

Zilla recovers from her gunshot sound, and Paul's trial is held. He is sentenced to three years in the State Penitentiary. Babbitt bids him goodbye at the railroad station, and then he suddenly realizes that without Paul, life has very little meaning for him.

During the next few months, Babbitt tries to keep himself busy in an effort to avoid thinking. Then, in June, Babbitt tries to organize a poker game, but he discovers that all his friends are busy. He realizes too that he doesn't want to play cards anyway. What he really wants is not a card game, nor wealth, or even social position. What he wants – and needs – is the friendship of Paul and the understanding and devotion of a woman, a woman like the fairy girl of his dreams. In the future, he decides, he will be a rebel and will do only what he really wants to do.

The next day at the club, however, Babbitt is not so rebellious as he is irritable. His friends tease him, but he is unresponsive. He continues to assert his new independence by going to the movies during business hours. Without admitting it to himself, Babbitt begins to seek female companionship – for this is what he really longs for. Unhappily, his advances to his stenographer, Miss McGoun, are unsuccessful. Later that week at a party, Babbitt attempts to befriend Louetta Swanson, having recalled her reputation as a flirt, but Louetta thinks that Babbitt is silly; she tells him that he's merely lonely for his wife.

Commentary

Heretofore, when Paul erred, Babbitt has always been able to be fairly effective at staying Paul's restlessness and, afterward, he could bask in proud tiredness after the ordeal was over. But now Paul has committed a crime, and Lewis' purpose is to show Babbitt's complete inability to comprehend what has happened. Paul is guilty; he shot Zilla through the shoulder with a real bullet from a real gun, and her wound is very bloody and real. Babbitt's code of behavior doesn't allow for such acts. He fears that Paul will be strangled in a quagmire of bureaucratic red tape before anyone realizes that Paul is not really bad. Likewise, Paul himself can scarcely believe what happened. In frustration, he simply pulled a trigger and a bullet cut through Zilla's shoulder. Paul tries to explain what happened, but his words sound like those of a retarded child.

Lewis tells us that from March to June, Babbitt kept busy in order to keep himself from "the bewilderment of thinking." Babbitt has always avoided real thinking, but especially now, he avoids thinking because thinking might involve reflecting, and reflecting might necessitate an evaluation of Paul's success in business and Paul's failure as a human being. After those subjects were considered, Babbitt would have to consider the value of his own life. Thus we watch Babbitt's unhappiness pile up around him. Once upon a time, Babbitt was happy not thinking; now it seems that Babbitt dare not think. Paul's astonishing act of revolt has unsettled Babbitt far more than he knows and, as he is soon to discover, games of bridge and evenings at the movies can't fill all of his leisure hours.

With Myra gone to visit relatives, Babbitt must create diversion, but Babbitt is not creative, and it is here that Lewis shows us a man about to become very frightened of being alone with himself. Sadly, Babbitt commits little crimes (a midnight raid on the ice box) in an attempt to understand what Paul has done; Babbitt hopes that even a small act of revolt will end his feelings of frustration. It does not; his anxiety remains.

Babbitt lusts for his dreamland fairy child, and he also lusts for a fairy child in the flesh. His spirits rise and fall erratically. He tries to flirt with his secretary and fails; he tries to make a pass at Louetta Swanson, grabbing at her as though grabbing for his lost youth. He believes that he is bestowing a gift of great value upon Louetta when he identifies her with the fairy child. In return, Louetta treats Babbitt like a little boy.

CHAPTER 24

Summary

Babbitt visits Paul at the penitentiary and sadly realizes that his friend's spirit is dead, even though there is life in his body. Babbitt also perceives that his own faith in the goodness of the world is dead. He unashamedly admits to himself that he is glad Myra is away.

One day, a very chic and sophisticated woman of Babbitt's age comes into his office to rent an apartment. Her name is Tanis Judique. Babbitt is charmed by her and decides to show her the rooms himself. He spends several hours with Tanis, behaving in his most suave manner. The two have many things in common, and they part on friendly terms. Afterward, Babbitt regrets that he did not develop their relationship further.

One of the manicurists in Babbitt's barber shop is a pretty young girl named Ida Putiak. For the first time, Babbitt notices that she is an attractive woman, and he makes a date with her. Later that week, he and Ida go to dinner together, but the girl is evidently not too stimulated by his company and, afterwards, she fights off his amorous advances. On his way home, Babbitt realizes that he is old enough to be Ida's father and that the poverty-stricken girl probably agreed to go out with him only in order to get a good meal. He is deeply ashamed of his foolish behavior.

Commentary

Babbitt's visit to the prison accomplishes an important change. After Babbitt leaves Paul, he accepts the reality of his friend's imprisonment. Paul and he have been parted and, whether or not it is just, Babbitt is soured on the world, on success, and on the quality of his own life. He feels dreadfully old and tired. We sense that money and success are no longer as satisfying as they once were. Besides material comfort, a man needs a friend—someone he can easily talk to, can relax with—someone who appreciates him. Paul filled that role for Babbitt. Now, with Paul behind prison walls and Myra far away with her relatives, Babbitt is adrift and must look for someone real to hang onto, someone with whom to begin a new, full relationship.

Propitiously, Tanis Judique—slender, fortyish, rosy-cheeked, and smartly dressed—is also looking for a certain something, but Tanis' quest is far simpler than Babbitt's. All she needs is an apartment. And since Babbitt deals in apartments and she in friendliness, the exchange is made. But Babbitt wants more. He pursues Tanis Judique with all the eagerness of an adolescent. He changes from being a disillusioned, aging businessman into a frisky gallant youngster, and we understand Babbitt's actions, even though Lewis makes them seem ridiculous. This is Babbitt's last fling before he surrenders to old age. He brags about being vice president of the Boosters' Club and having a man's responsibility in the "world's work." He orders elevator boys about as if he were nobility. In his awkward way, although he doesn't realize it, Babbitt is asking this pretty woman to look at him, to tell him that he is still handsome, that she needs him and that she loves him.

Tanis Judique's attentiveness sparks Babbitt's zeal so keenly that Babbitt methodically decides to "practice" his newly stirring masculinity on the manicure girl at the Pompeian Barber Shop. But if Babbitt seemed bumbling in the scene with Tanis, in this scene he is ludicrous and then, finally, pitiful. He "quakes" before the manicurist; he speaks jerkily and is forced to date her in a taxi; then, as a reward, he is kissed and patted readily and mechanically. He has exchanged the price of a dinner for the manicurist's easy intimacy. The confidence which Babbitt had when he left Tanis Judique is gone.

CHAPTERS 25–26

Summary

In the morning, Babbitt awakens cheerfully. He reconsiders his behavior of the past few weeks and debates whether or not to continue his "rebellion." He resolves to go on seeking, but promises himself that he will discontinue his futile chasing after girls. In August, Myra comes back to Zenith, but Babbitt has not missed her. He dreads being alone with her, but he tries his best to seem enthusiastic about her return.

As a result, Babbitt decides to spend his vacation alone in the Maine woods where he and Paul had such a peaceful time the year before. He hopes to be able to rejuvenate his spirit there. He tells his wife that he is going to New York on a business trip.

At Lake Sunasquam, he seeks out the company of the Indian

guides, hoping to discover through them the freedom and content-ment of a virile, outdoor life. He is disappointed to learn, however, that they are crass and materialistic men—just like those whom he left behind in Zenith. Even worse, the woods are not the same without Paul. One night, Babbitt begins to understand that he can never escape Zenith; the Zenith way of life is deeply imprinted on his mind and soul. He still does not comprehend what he is seeking, but he knows that there is only one place where he can really find it. A day or so later, he boards the train for home.

On the train to Zenith, Babbitt encounters Seneca Doane, with whom he had been friendly in college. They speak together for the rest of the trip, and Babbitt is surprised to discover that Doane is not the revolutionary monster that he has been portrayed to be by the conservative businessmen of Zenith. Babbitt agrees with some of Doane's beliefs and begins to feel like a fledgling idealist.

A few hours after his arrival in Zenith, Babbitt calls on Zilla Ries-ling. She now lives in a cheap boarding house in a poor neighborhood. He is surprised to see how her physical appearance has changed and is shocked to learn that she has become intolerantly religious. She has no mercy for Paul and refuses to cooperate in an effort to get him a pardon.

At the Athletic Club, Babbitt defends Seneca Doane when the attorney is bad-mouthed by the members. Otherwise, Babbitt's life continues in its usual fashion.

Commentary

Babbitt's actions—which once were compulsively and obsessively consistent—have now become inconsistent. Babbitt the solid citizen realizes that a change has occurred and also realizes that nothing has been gained by his rebellion, but he has no answer. He knows only that he must continue his rebellion. He knows that what he is doing is impractical, but he cannot help himself. He searched for peace in the Maine woods with Paul, and he was content for awhile; he was happy when he returned to Zenith and began speaking out in behalf of his fellow realtors and promoting a successful campaign for Mayor Prout. The vice presidency of the Boosters' Club was a unique thrill. Yet Babbitt feels lost.

When Babbitt returns again to the Maine woods, it is as though he is looking for something lost; somewhere, somehow, he missed the opportunity to be happy. Babbitt determines to find a new life for himself in this basic, uncomplicated backwoods frontier. Yet he knows that this ideal is futile. Once committed to a wife, to children, and to a business firm, one must assume continuous responsibility. But at the same time, the confused child in Babbitt reasons that because he feels less of a man in the city, he can be more of a man here in the woods, where he can shed the comforts and the complexities of civilization.

Lewis notes that Babbitt approaches Joe Paradise's shack as though it were a "real home"; then he shows us the emptiness of Babbitt's homecoming. The rest of the chapter is structured with irony as Joe Paradise greets Babbitt unenthusiastically, then lackadaisically accepts Babbitt's request for a guide and reluctantly agrees to walk Babbitt to the camp site. Babbitt's idea of "real living" is squelched by Joe Paradise's confession that for sixteen years he has traveled to the camp grounds by motorboat and that, if he had a lot of money, he would open up a "swell" shoe store.

Once again, one of Babbitt's dreams eludes him. Not only is he depressed, but he is also plagued by worries about what is going on in Zenith. In a rare moment of insight into himself, he realizes that he is a Zenith citizen, a successful realtor, and a man who can never run away from himself. As trite as it sounds, Babbitt's discovery excites him. He vows to do something with his new knowledge. But we have heard him make vows before.

After the frustrating and empty Maine woods experience, Babbitt feels emotionally and spiritually depleted and is ready to grasp any hand that suggests friendship. With his usual fine sense of irony, Lewis arranges for that hand to belong to Seneca Doane – a socialist and, therefore, an archenemy of the Babbitt whom we met at the beginning of the novel. Here, Doane reveals a new side of Babbitt to himself, and, as a result, Babbitt becomes more confused than ever. In his college days, Doane reminds him, Babbitt was determined to be a lawyer who championed the poor, one who would take their cases for nothing. Here again, we are reminded of the duality within Babbitt, the dichotomy between what he was before he became a smug and financially well-off Booster and what he is today.

Doane reveals something startling to Babbitt, and Babbitt picks it up and thinks that it might be the key he has been searching for.

Heretofore, socialism has always been suspect – a dirty word – yet Doane is not dirty. Doane is a humanitarian. So goes Babbitt's reasoning process. Of course, Babbitt is not completely converted by Doane's talk about the past, yet when Doane drops the name Lord Wycombe, Babbitt suddenly reasons that one can be a socialist and also a friend to the rich and lordly. Instantly, he is ready to accept a new political label for himself.

Babbitt's enthusiasm with his new set of quasi-liberal views needs a practice run, and so Babbitt visits Zilla Riesling. Earlier, like Doane, Zilla was an enemy of Babbitt. Lewis aligns these former enemies of Babbitt on either side of the new Babbitt. We see that Babbitt found Doane to be a far different man inside than Babbitt suspected. Now Babbitt likewise finds Zilla to be a far different woman than the shrew Babbitt believed her to be. In fact, Zilla is almost unrecognizable to Babbitt. She is poor now, she looks old, and age is ugly on her in a way that frightens Babbitt.

Babbitt cannot cope with Zilla; now she is "vicious in the name of virtue" and damns Paul and bares Babbitt's worse faults to himself. In contrast, Seneca Doane presents Babbitt with a new suit of political thought, and Zilla rips it – and Babbitt – to shreds. Babbitt's attempt to be kind and "liberal" to Zilla fails.

CHAPTERS 27–28

Summary

Late in September, a major strike takes place in Zenith. It begins with a walkout of telephone company employees, and they are soon joined by truck drivers and dairy product workers. Many other unions act in sympathy with them and, before long, the city rings with talk of a general strike. Most business and industry in Zenith is almost at a standstill. Everyone in the city feels compelled to take sides in this dispute because the strike is bitter. There are many street demonstrations and fights between strikers and scabs. A fire in one of the closed factories is blamed on the workers. Seneca Doane is one of the few prominent citizens to stand up for the strikers, and he defends a number of them in court. Not surprisingly, all of Babbitt's friends and associates angrily oppose the workers.

One Sunday, Dr. Drew delivers a sermon against the strike.

Babbitt questions the wisdom of the pastor's outlook and arouses the suspicions of his friends. Later on, at the Athletic Club, Babbitt speaks out in behalf of an objective evaluation of the issues. His friends begin to grow alarmed.

Eventually, the National Guard is called out to maintain order. Since the officers and most of the enlisted men are from the conservative class, the strikers often receive harsh treatment. Babbitt protests this brutality, claiming that the striking workers are not bomb throwers or revolutionaries, and that they are entitled to their right to protest. Later on, Babbitt is seen attending a leftist street meeting. His cronies begin to fear that he is becoming a radical.

Myra and the children do not understand Babbitt's political change. They are confused, and likewise, Babbitt himself is confused. He is not a socialist nor a traitor to his class. He is only trying to stand up for fair play and mutual understanding. He wishes he had someone to discuss his problems with.

One afternoon, Tanis Judique calls Babbitt's office to inquire about some repairs to her apartment. Babbitt decides to take care of the matter personally, and so he goes to see her. When he gets there, they have a cup of tea and soon grow chummy. He tells her about some of his problems, including the scandal about Paul and Zilla and the continuing reaction of his friends to his attitude during the recent strike. Tanis is sympathetic and understanding; she admires his courage. Babbitt brags about his business and social achievements, and she appears impressed. Before long, they start to address each other by their first names and begin to grow affectionate. Babbitt telephones his wife and tells her that he has to work late; he is, of course, going to have dinner with Tanis and spend most of the evening in her apartment. In her presence, he feels a serenity and a confidence that he has not felt in months.

Commentary

Until now, Babbitt's values have been tested only in relatively minor skirmishes; Verona and Ted's behavior has put him on the defensive and certain important social dinner parties have turned out badly. Until Paul Riesling's rash act, Babbitt has never faced such a dramatic moral crisis as Zenith's labor population deciding to strike.

A year ago, Babbitt would have denounced the strike as traitorous socialism, but he can no longer respond with such an instant evaluation. Babbitt's newfound liberalism has not matured sufficiently so that he can feel completely comfortable with it; yet, at the same time, he senses that his old "sound and sane" politics are selfish and hateful. Dr. Drew, for instance, whose phrases Babbitt used to repeat so glibly, is now dismissed by Babbitt. Suddenly, Babbitt realizes that Dr. Drew's calling the strike an "untoward series of industrial dislocations" is nothing but pompous rot. Babbitt becomes so suspect that Chum Frink and Verg Gunch begin acting like secret police, watching Babbitt as carefully as the National Guardsmen are watching Zenith's rioters.

One of Lewis' ways of showing us Babbitt's character is by showing us what or who impresses Babbitt. At present, Babbitt is impressed by Seneca Doane's and Professor Brockbank's participation in the workers' march. When he is at the Athletic Club, Babbitt no longer gives instant lip service to the ultra-conservative element that would like to annihilate any dissenting mob. Babbitt cannot see the strikers as abstractions or unpenned animals.

The psychologically exhausting dilemma of taking either the side of the workers or that of management makes Babbitt easy prey for Tanis Judique. Her name is exotic; she wears fluttering black chiffon, and she has an apartment with a view. She offers escape to Babbitt and he accepts her offer. Babbitt's ego expands, and as the chapter closes, Babbitt is arranging the scene for his seduction of Tanis – a cottage fireplace and streaming rain outside – everything chosen as though it were taking place in a dream, a state of mind in which Babbitt is most at peace.

CHAPTER 29

Summary

Tanis Judique's friendship strengthens Babbitt's resolution. At the club and elsewhere, he continues to be critical of many generally accepted beliefs. Some of his friends consider him a crank, but a few, like Vergil Gunch, seem seriously concerned about Babbitt's radicalism.

Babbitt soon begins to spend all his free time with Tanis and thinks of her constantly when they are apart. Furthermore, whenever he compares the chic Tanis with the dumpy Myra, his wife comes out second best. At times, Myra's comments or behavior make him feel guilty, and he often resolves to spend more time with her, but his longing for Tanis usually triumphs, and he hastens to join his lover.

Tanis is one of a group of bohemians who call themselves "The Bunch." This group has frequent late parties, where the members spend their time dancing wildly and drinking heavily. Babbitt learns to be one of them and adopts many of their habits, although his morning hangovers and fatigue serve as unheeded warnings that he is too old for this sort of lifestyle.

Myra leaves to take care of a sick relative in another town, and Babbitt takes advantage of her absence to become even more involved in his new social life. After awhile, he becomes less discreet about his relationship with Tanis and her friends. Once, while they are drunk, they encounter Professor Pumphrey, and another time Babbitt and Tanis are seen together in a downtown restaurant by Vergil Gunch. Babbitt soon becomes the subject of whispered gossip and public scandal. This troubles him, as does his realization that he is growing unhappy with the conventions and demands of the Bunch.

One day, Gunch comes to Babbitt's office to advise him about the formation of a local chapter of the Good Citizens' League. This is an organization dedicated to fighting socialism and liberalism, although it maintains a camouflage over its activities by professing an interest in such civic matters as park and city planning. Naturally, all of the respectable members of the community are joining, and Gunch invites Babbitt.

Babbitt feels that he must assert his independence; he refuses to commit himself. Gunch becomes indignant and warns Babbitt that in the struggle between decency and Americanism on the one hand and red tyranny on the other, everyone must take sides. The League, he says, considers anyone who does not join to be an enemy. That night, Babbitt worries fearfully about the consequences of his behavior.

Commentary

There are two schools of thought about the newly emerging George F. Babbitt. To his fellow club members, Babbitt has, inexplicably, become a "crank," while Babbitt thinks of himself as possibly a highly original man: successful, conservative, yet touched with wisdom. He sees himself as a courageous pioneer — one who crosses social strata in the name of decency. And in addition to Babbitt's new belief in humanity, he has a beautiful and usually discreet lady love. With Myra gone, Babbitt realizes that he will be free to spend more time with Tanis, but, ironically, the sense of adventure and daring that once surrounded his affair with Tanis Judique soon dissolves.

Babbitt's illusions about Tanis begin to crumble when Tanis' crowd of friends increasingly invades their idyllic love life. Babbitt feels like an alien. The men in Tanis' Bunch are not successful, and the women are not lovely like Tanis. As an alien, Babbitt looks at the scene from a distance and sees the crowd trying too hard to have fun – drinking too much, gossiping too loudly, and dancing too wildly – and he sees himself trying too hard to follow their steps.

Despite this insight, however, Babbitt buys a yellow tie – not to boost his spirits, but to look younger – in order to look more like one of the Bunch. He has begun to replace "old" things; he has a new play-wife, a new group of friends, and now he has new, if often disturbing ideas that are eroding the old solid citizen mold.

Ultimately, though, Babbitt is unable to break completely with his solid citizen past and give himself completely to a new, if dubious, future with Tanis and her Bunch. Similarly, Babbitt is unable to endorse the Good Citizens' League. Not long ago, Babbitt would have been the biggest booster of the League – but at that time, he would have been endorsing the League simply because of its name: the Good Citizens' League. Now, Babbitt can discern that the League isn't concerned with "good citizens." Its aim is to enforce conformity. There is no room in the League for dissenting opinion. Babbitt realizes that the world is no longer divided into two groups – the good citizens and the bad citizens. Life is complex; it cannot be divided into two groups – the red-blooded all-American middle class vs. the socialists.

CHAPTERS 30–31

Summary

When Myra returns home, Babbitt tries his best to be attentive and warm. He finds it difficult, however, to restrain his impatience and irritability when he is in Myra's company. He is torn between wanting to be a good husband and also wanting to continue his relationship with Tanis and her friends.

Babbitt reassesses his wife in the light of all that has happened, and he discovers, to his surprise, that she too is an individual and a worthwhile human being. This realization, though, does not ease the situation. The Babbitts have frequent disagreements. One Sunday afternoon, Myra induces him to come to a meeting of the American New Thought League. Babbitt attends, but is far less inspired than she anticipated. After the meeting, they quarrel violently. Myra accuses him of having become callous and inconsiderate. Babbitt guiltily denies the charge, and he pities her bewilderment. He begins to wonder whether his new way of life has any real value, and to what end it will lead him. Thus, he apologizes to Myra and silently vows not to see Tanis anymore.

During the next few days, Babbitt strictly adheres to his decision. Tanis telephones him at the office, but his responses are brusque and vague. She writes him a letter and asks him to pay her a visit. Babbitt does not want to go, but he finally keeps the appointment.

At Tanis' apartment, she asks Babbitt's forgiveness for anything she may have done to offend him, but it is too late. Babbitt sees her now as a foolish middle-aged woman who no longer attracts him. He does not dislike her, but sees no point in continuing their relationship. Despite her pleas, Babbitt bids Tanis farewell and leaves.

Commentary

Babbitt wonders if it might be easier to keep his vows, to stay home and behave himself if Myra were not at her sister's. Clearly, Babbitt is still confused; he would like to "play around . . . yet not make a fool" of himself. Alternatives seems to be either black or white; either he's a good citizen—law-abiding and spotless—or else he's a libertine. Babbitt is struggling for a life that is comfortable and available between these extremes. This need to transcend pigeon-holed categories and create a gray area for his existence is painfully revolutionary for Babbitt.

Likewise, Myra reveals a new dimension of herself, one which we have never seen before. For whatever reason, Myra rebels: she is tried of planning meals, tired of cooking and sewing, tired of being Babbitt's wife and Ted and Verona's mother, and tired of trying to save pennies day after day after day.

Babbitt feels guilty when he argues with Myra, but he feels proud that he has not seen Tanis for ten days. His pride does not last long; he flees to Tanis because of business worries, Myra's whining, and the children's troubles. He comes "home" to Tanis—only to be confronted with Tanis' own barrage of troubles. Eventually, he is able to escape from Tanis and breathe the sweet air of freedom. Ironically, Babbitt is far from free. Tanis has her claim on him—as do Myra, Ted, Verona, and the Zenith Athletic Club. Babbitt used to be the same man to all of them: he was George F. Babbitt, solid citizen and Booster. Now he is a stranger to them and to himself.

CHAPTER 32

Summary

On his return home, Babbitt finds Myra waiting for him. An argument ensues, during which Babbitt boldly announces that he has been seeing another woman—drinking and doing all sorts of forbidden things. He justifies his actions by accusing Myra and all the other respectable people around him of being unimaginative bores. Myra admits that she may be partly at fault and she ends up apologizing to him for her deficiencies. Babbitt feels greatly relieved and satisfied at this development.

At the Boosters' Club luncheon that week, a reactionary senator delivers a speech about his recent trip to Europe. Many of his statements are ignorant and bigoted. Babbitt criticizes his opinion on immigration and other matters, to the disgust of many of the other members. Later that day, a committee from the Good Citizens' League, made up of Charlie McKelvey and two other influential businessmen, calls on Babbitt. They deliver an ultimatum: either Babbitt join the League at once and support its policies or he will suffer the consequences. Babbitt tries to make them understand that his political and economic ideas are in accord with theirs, but he is not convincing. The League representatives demand that he join, but some perverse instinct will not allow Babbitt to agree to join. He feels that he must assert himself at all costs. He rejects their offer even though he is terribly frightened of what may happen.

Babbitt soon learns the consequences of his refusal to join the Good Citizens' League; all of Zenith's responsible and influential people stop talking to him. He is cold-shouldered even by old friends like Vergil Gunch and Eathorne. At home, Myra suggests that perhaps he should join the League, but Babbitt refuses. He is not at peace, however, with his decision.

In the next few days, Babbitt begins to lose customers, and some of his most faithful employees resign. The Street Traction Company, for which he has done profitable work, gives its most current business to a rival realtor. Wherever Babbitt goes, people whisper about him or watch him silently, and still no one speaks to him. The strain on him is unbearable; he longs to return to the path of respectability and conformity. He is even willing to join the League – but only if he can do so with dignity.

In his confusion, Babbitt tries to see Tanis, but she too is cold and unfriendly. His wife does not fully understand the situation and cannot help him. He has no one else to turn to. Babbitt's only support comes from Ted, who is home on a visit, and Eunice Littlefield. The two young people praise Babbitt for being so courageous and such a troublemaker, but they view his behavior as a kind of prank, not as a serious assertion of principle.

Commentary

Babbitt's confrontation with Myra concerning Tanis is quiet. She knew about the affair and, no doubt, rehearsed a scene of furious revelation; when the blow-up came, however, she was too tired and too relieved to quarrel. Instead of quarreling about Tanis, they argue about Babbitt's being an old "stick-in-the-mud." The scene is brief, and both Myra and Babbitt go to bed pleased. Again a scene ends with Babbitt making a promise to himself; this time, he promises to run his own life.

Next day, Babbitt cannot remember his reasons for not wanting to join the Good Citizens' League when he is approached by three members of the committee. But Babbitt refuses to join the League and, for a short while, he does "run his own life." Babbitt's resolve is literally bankrupted when money begins to flow out of Babbitt's real estate business and into those of his competitors. He walks in fear; he feels like an outcast. His pride binds him; he wants the League to make an overture to him. He wants an honorable peace with it. Ted and Eunice are the only people who admire Babbitt's backing Seneca Doane; to them, Babbitt is a much-needed voice of reason and compassion in prejudiced, conservative Zenith. The two young people make Babbitt feel more secure, but out on the street, in broad daylight, he feels fearfully alone. He feels the glare of critical eyes and hears whispered, conspiratorial voices.

CHAPTERS 33–34

Summary

One night Babbitt lies awake, bemoaning his fate. He chastises himself for having lost Tanis; he is sorry that his relationship with his wife is such a poor one. He recognizes that he and Myra have no chance for a reconciliation unless he ends his rebellion against conformity, but his pride will not allow him to be bullied into changing his views.

About three o'clock that morning, Babbitt discovers that his wife is ill. He tries to help her, but Myra's abdominal pains continue to increase. Terrified, Babbitt calls the doctor. When he arrives, the physician gives Myra a sedative and promises to return the following day. Babbitt sits at his wife's bedside all night, holding her hand and frantically hoping for her recovery.

In the morning, the doctor returns, accompanied by a specialist. After a brief examination, they announce that the patient has acute appendicitis and that an immediate operation is required. Myra has an old-fashioned fear of hospitals and becomes very upset. Babbitt stays with her in the ambulance and in her room, cheering her up, pleading for her forgiveness and affirming that he loves her. To his great joy, the operation is a success. Afterwards, Babbitt determines to return to a normal way of life. He visits Myra every day at the hospital, and, together, they review all their past mistakes and make plans for the future.

To Babbitt's surprise, the Gunches and the Littlefields, as well as other old friends, are concerned about Myra and visit her at the hospital. They behave in a friendly manner toward Babbitt also. People on the street and the Athletic Club often ask about her, and he begins to appreciate the warm and genuine human values of the world he was fighting against. When Gunch casually asks him to join the League, Babbitt eagerly accepts.

Within a few weeks, Babbitt has regained his old position in the community. Once more, he is an active and vocal spokesman of the red-blooded middle-class way of life; once more, he is a vocal opponent of Seneca Doane, labor unions, immigrants, and immorality.

Meanwhile, the Good Citizens' League spreads throughout the country, making inroads into other commercial cities similar to Zenith. All the prosperous citizens and business leaders become members, devoting themselves to the establishment of solid, middle-class American life. In Zenith, Babbitt takes an active part in all these activities, and, not surprisingly, he soon regains the esteem of his old friends. He returns to his church, even though he is never completely convinced of the wisdom of Dr. Drew. Most of all, Babbitt takes pleasure once more in attending all the meetings and social affairs of the Elks, the Boosters, and the Athletic Club.

Everything returns to normal. Verona and Escott are married, and the Street Traction Company allows Babbitt to handle its next crooked real-estate deal.

During a vacation weekend, Ted and Eunice are secretly married, and Ted make plans to leave the university in order to take a better-paying factory job. When the two families involved learn about the wedding, they are shocked and irate. Everyone vehemently opposes the actions of the two rash young people. Babbitt speaks to Ted privately, however, and promises to support the boy's decision. He does not approve of having Ted's incomplete education or of his early marriage, but, Babbitt says, at least Ted is doing what he really wants to do. The most important thing, Babbitt says, is to be unafraid of the conventions and influences of the outside world and to do what one sees as the right course for himself. Babbitt says that he is sorry that he learned this lesson so late in his own life.

Commentary

Ironically, it is whiny old Myra and her appendicitis operation which cause Babbitt's restoration. Myra, the woman whom Babbitt felt to be old and unlovely, changes into an invalid, absolutely dependent on Babbitt. A part of Babbitt, wedded to him for more than twenty years, Myra has been injured inside by an unseen something. She is afraid; she is no longer the nagging mother figure Babbitt battled every day; now she is a frightened-eyed child, needing Babbitt's love and reassurance.

Myra Babbitt, brought down mysteriously, is George Babbitt's salvation, and like the Prodigal Son, Babbitt is warmly greeted back into the conservative fold by Verg Gunch and the members of Babbitt's old gang as they visit Myra in the hospital. Babbitt's shoulder is patted in sympathy, and old differences disappear. Babbitt returns to the solid citizen mold and he finally becomes a solid member of the Good Citizens' League.

Accordingly, big money returns to the coffers of Babbitt's real-estate business, and so the cycle of Babbitt's security, his loss of security, and his security regained comes full circle. From being one of the club, to one of Tanis' Bunch, Babbitt returns to being one of the club again.

Restored to membership in Zenith's moneymaking fraternity, Babbitt rotely endorses the notion that America's world-famous equality means absolute conformity — conformity in thought and dress and manners. Conformity is solid gospel to Zenith's bank presidents, landowners, corporation lawyers, fashionable doctors, and realtors. In other words, America's "equality" has nothing to do with equal opportunities or equal education.

As a final satirical touch, Lewis creates a ceremonial scene honoring George F. Babbitt's restoration. Babbitt's peers, the Zenith Boosters, give him their greatest honor: good-naturedly and with mock seriousness, they make fun of him. They tease him about his middle name — Follansbee. There is much hooting about the name being prissy but, by such inverse humor, Babbitt is sure that once again he is considered to be a man — one of the boys. He no longer will have to desperately say to himself that he is "free" or that he is "going to run his own life". Now he can say that he is going to run things to "suit himself." "Suiting himself," of course, means conforming to the middle-class lifestyle and to the values of men like himself. Babbitt has whimpered his last; he has accepted old age, old Myra, old friends, and all the old conservative platitudes of Zenith's mens clubs.

As for young Ted's eloping with Eunice Littlefield, Myra and Verona and the Littlefields are "properly shocked" by the young people's daring. Yet it is Babbitt who silences their protests. He ushers Ted into the dining room and confesses that he doesn't really approve of early marriage, but that he does approve of Eunice. Thus, Babbitt bequeaths his dream to Ted — to become whatever he sets out to become. If Ted's ambition lies in mechanics, then Babbitt, disappointed but proud, will support his son's determination. So far, Ted has grabbed the girl he wanted without ceremony. There seems to be some hope that Ted will be more independent than his father was —

independent of a good neighborhood, the right friends, and deadening conformity.

CHARACTER ANALYSIS

GEORGE F. BABBITT

What is George F. Babbitt really like? What kind of a man is he beneath the swagger, the ready handshake, and the expensive clothes? We are never sure, just as Babbitt is never sure – because there is only a small remnant of a vital human being beneath Babbitt's surface.

Beneath Babbitt's exterior, there is a vague nervousness and comfortableness – a temporary nausea, caused by Babbitt's ebbing intelligence, imagination, and integrity. And when the novel ends, Babbitt says that he feels fine and healthy, and to all appearances he is, but the reader knows that Babbitt's last dregs of intelligence, imagination, and integrity have been distilled into the essence of what is known today as "Babbittry."

To be a Babbitt or to be guilty of Babbittry is to behave like George F. Babbitt. It means that in one's private life one should, like Babbitt, read the morning paper and, then, computerlike, store up opinions from the editorial pages to regurgitate later with business associates when it is necessary to impress someone or settle arguments. Babbitt has few opinions of his own; his opinions are articulated by other people. Parroting editorials is Babbitt's way of learning, of acquiring wisdom.

Memorizing phrases and attitudes of politically conversative editorials is done every morning, by rote, over coffee. It is one of Babbitt's daily rituals, similar to his lovemaking – except that his lovemaking is a ritual rarely and only disinterestedly performed. Babbitt's wife is a noisy presence, a housekeeper, and a cook; Myra Babbitt is no longer the lovely or mysterious woman whom Babbitt married. She is Babbitt's domestic anchor and also a millstone around his neck. Babbitt and Myra rarely talk about important matters. They talk on the surface about such things as material possessions and costly knickknacks; this is the substance of their common ground.

Lewis make little attempt to plot Babbitt's actions for us. He simply presents scenes: A Day in the Life of George F. Babbitt; the Babbitts Entertain with Cocktails and Dinner; Babbitt Plays at Politics; Babbitt Helps the Church; Babbitt and his Children Together; Babbitt and his Best Friend, Paul; The Short-lived Rebellion of Babbitt; and, finally, Babbitt Regained. Other than Babbitt's recurring discontent, there is little conflict in the novel. There is usually only Lewis' voice, leading us like a satiric tour guide through Babbitt's follies. Repeatedly, we see Babbitt's vast pride in American business and American big bucks and his belief that moneymaking automatically equates with Progress. Simultaneously, like subtitles, Lewis' comments mimic loud, smug, conservative Midwesterners and their "my-country-right-or-wrong" attitudes.

Sinclair Lewis has written an exposé, a highly critical social document showing (and exaggerating) how Americans of a certain Midwestern ilk behave, talk, and amass unnecessary material objects. It has been said that Lewis showed Americans "what they are really like" but he does not; *Babbitt* shows Americans what they are like at their most mediocre.

CRITICAL ESSAY

TECHNIQUE AND CONTENT IN *BABBITT*

From a strictly technical point of view, Sinclair Lewis is deficient as a writer in a number of ways. During his lifetime, many critics — particularly those who were unable to endorse his vision of America — attacked him for his lack of artistry. Others, more sympathetic to Lewis' message, took the opposing position and refused to acknowledge any flaws in his technique. Needless to say, both groups of critics were wrong, although some of their specific evaluations were indeed correct. Now the furor surrounding Lewis is long gone, and it is possible to look at his writing technique and the content of his novels with more objectivity.

Most of Sinclair Lewis' faults as a writer are the result of a tendency toward immoderation and overstatement. Lewis is frequently carried away by his enthusiasm for his subject or for rhetorical devices, and he often forgets to restrain himself artistically. As a result, the same characteristics of his style may be praised or blamed, depending on the degree to which they are present in the examples selected for study.

For instance, Lewis often uses irony effectively and skillfully to emphasize his meaning and to help delineate character, as in the line, "Babbitt loved his mother, and sometimes he rather liked her . . ." On other occasions, however, as in the mechanical juxtapositioning of the dinner for the McKelveys with the dinner given by the Over-brooks, the comparison of events is significant, but the irony is over-simplified and artificial. Likewise, Lewis' pleasure with rhetoric now and then escapes the bounds of objectivity, and he ends up sounding like a neighborhood gossip. Lewis' descriptions are always humorous – if one enjoys sarcasm.

For example, Lewis writes, "His shoes were black-laced boots, good boots, honest boots, standard boots, extraordinarily uninteresting boots." Lewis, of course, isn't really interested in the boots; he's characterizing Babbitt as good, honest, straight-laced, and "extraordinarily uninteresting." In contrast to this gossipy, sarcastic tone, Lewis can also swing to an opposite stylistic extreme – that of the syrupy, oversentimental writer. For example, he describes Babbitt's adolescent-like dreams of the fairy girl as being "more romantic than scarlet pagodas by a silver sea."

Clearly, Lewis has a brilliant ear for the spoken language of the 1920s and a great talent for mimicry. Some of his vocal reproductions and exaggerations of colloquial speech patterns are among the novel's most memorable and amusing passages. Through his aping of native speech patterns, Lewis demonstrates the empty and unimaginative quality of middle-class American thought and, at the same time, he teases us with rich humor. The dullness and vapidity of the way that the characters in Babbitt communicate and express themselves empha-sizes all of Lewis' intense feelings about their beliefs, backgrounds, and lack of sophistication.

It has been charged, and with some truth, that Lewis sometimes overused slang and was too extravagant in the length and volume of his imitations, and that as a result, the language of his characters sometimes seems stilted and unreal. That is a danger faced by every novelist who depends on colloquial language to give "life" and "local color" to his novel.

An additional factor in an evaluation of Babbitt is a considera-tion of the novel's unusual structure. Instead of being a traditional novel in which the adventures and personal evolution of an individual are shown in detail and traced over a period of time, *Babbitt* is a col-lection of nearly thirty separate episodes. Each of these vignettes deals with a different aspect of life in the early Prohibition era, and they are given a unity only by the constant presence of George F. Babbitt. All of these short pieces have their own structural integrity, but they are arranged in a haphazard fashion. Their order could be changed, and their number could be added to or subtracted from without affecting the development of the novel or changing its ultimate outcome.

Taken together, these vignettes give us a thorough picture of middle-class American life and culture in the period Lewis was writing about. The use of these topical pieces radically loosens the framework of the novel and weakens it as a balanced artistic construction. On the other hand, all of these episodes have a strong documentary flavor; each of them accurately depicts a particular segment of American life. The use of this device strengthens the impression that *Babbitt* is a truthful and dependable report on American mores and thus heightens its value as a social document.

It should also be mentioned that while many of the characters in *Babbitt* are caricatures and representative types, they are drawn in such a realistic and skillful manner that the reader rarely notices this flaw. Fortunately, a few characters in the novel, such as Paul Riesling, are sufficiently full-blooded to arouse real sympathy and interest.

Babbitt, the protagonist, sometimes seems slightly unreal, for he is such a stereotype and personification of the cliched middle-class, Midwestern, polyester businessman. Babbitt is limited in the options open to him at any point since he usually acts as a representative of a certain class of man. At the same time, his loneliness and yearnings, as well as his vague sense of unhappy aimlessness are typical of modern man's dilemma; thus, many people can readily identify with Babbitt. As a result, despite his many personal defects and partly because of his stereotyped image, Babbitt has become in many ways an archetypal figure in the modern American mythos. Because Babbitt symbolizes the fear and pain of the individual made captive by a huge, commercial and industrial mass society, he has achieved a niche in our country's imagination and consciousness. Babbitt is the quintessential middle-class mediocre man; we see him trying to break the seams of mediocrity's straitjacket — and failing. Some people, of course, endorse mediocrity. Nebraska's former senator Roman Hruskra said that he supported a particular nominee to the Supreme Court because the mediocre people of this nation need a representative on the Supreme Court bench.

Clearly, *Babbitt* was written before the Vietnam War. It was written during an era when the United States had suddenly discovered that it was a major world political power and that its industrial, financial, and military might were unsurpassed. Following World War I, a wave of prosperity and self-confidence swept the nation. The vast majority of American people developed an egotistical belief in the superiority of themselves and their institutions. In the 1920s, America was chauvinistic, smug, intolerant, reactionary, and materialistic. It had contempt for anything foreign and, in its search for conformity, it distrusted and opposed anything unfamiliar or new. The strongest citadel of these narrow-minded beliefs was the Midwest, where Lewis grew up.

Lewis was a sensitive and perceptive observer of his fellow countrymen and their way of life. He proudly recognized his nation's legitimately great achievements, and he sensed the country's potential for even further greatness. However, he was also aware of America's rich democratic and spiritual heritage; he understood the value of respect and consideration for other peoples and other ways of life.

Throughout all his novels, Lewis attempts to expose the worst defects of America in the hope that he can warn his countrymen while there is still time. His satire is often brutal and bitter, and he made many enemies and offended people. He is sometimes guilty of injustice, exaggeration, disrespect, and lack of gratitude, but, nonetheless, for the first time, an American author tried to show his countrymen what they were really like under the surface of their lives. Through Lewis' efforts, and those writers and thinkers who were influenced by him, some of this country's worst failings were eventually rectified. While reading his novels, one notes that some of his criticisms are still relevant. This reaction is proof of how accurate and on-target Lewis' observations were.

Sinclair Lewis was one of the most profound and astute students of America in the twentieth century. He created an image of our national civilization to which Americans will always be obligated to compare themselves. He communicated his message with clarity, precision, and accuracy, and in a form that attracted a wide and varied audience. Few satirists have ever been able to do better.

SUGGESTED ESSAY TOPICS

1. Lewis' structure of *Babbitt*
2. Aspects of American home life satirized by Lewis
3. Babbitt as a caricature
4. The "dull" things in Babbitt's life
5. Lewis' attitude toward Myra Babbitt
6. Lewis' feelings about Midwestern morality
7. Babbitt: a hypocrite or an honest man?
8. Lewis' portrait of Zenith: accurate or inaccurate?
9. Lewis' parody of Tanis Judique and her bohemian friends
10. Lewis' attitude toward Seneca Doane
11. The friendship between Paul Riesling and Babbitt
12. Characteristics of Lewis' writing style

SELECTED BIBLIOGRAPHY

COMMAGER, HENRY STEELE. *The American Mind.* New Haven: 1950.

GEISMAR, MAXWELL. *The Last of the Provincials: The American Novel, 1915–1925.* New York: 1949.

GREBSTEIN, SHELDON N. *Sinclair Lewis.* New York: 1962.

HICKS, GRANVILLE. "Sinclair Lewis and the Good Life," *English Journal,* College Edition, XXV (1936).

HORTON, THOMAS D. "Sinclair Lewis: The Symbol of an Era," *North American Review*, CCXLVII (1940).

SCHORER, MARK. *Sinclair Lewis.* University of Minnesota Pamphlets on American Writers, Minneapolis: 1963.

_____. *Sinclair Lewis, An American Life.* New York: 1961.

_____, ed. *Sinclair Lewis: A Collection of Critical Essays.* Englewood Cliffs, N.J.: 1962.

VAN DOREN, CARL. *Sinclair Lewis, A Biographical Sketch.* New York: 1933.